WINTALITY

-Unlock Your Success DNA-

by Baylor Barbee

To have a creative mind,
Read Chapter 9, I
can relate to you as
a creative!

Excited to see
you thrive.

B/B

CORNELLSTREET

▮▮▮▬▬▬ PUBLISHING ▬▬▮▮▮

214.325.2234

WINTALITY: Unlock Your Success DNA

Copyright © 2016 by Baylor Barbee

Cover Design: Cornell Street Publishing

All rights reserved. No part of this publication may be reproduced, distributed, or transmitted in any form or by any means, including photocopying, recording, or other electronic or mechanical methods, without the prior written permission of the publisher, except in the case of brief quotations embodied in critical reviews and certain other noncommercial uses permitted by copyright law.

For permission requests, write to the publisher, addressed "Attention: Permissions Coordinator," at the address below.

Cornell Street Publishing
4447 N Central Expressway
STE 110-201
Dallas, TX 75205
www.cornellstreet.com
publisher@cornellstreet.com

Special discounts are available on quantity purchases by corporations, associations, and others.

For details, contact the publisher at the address above.

ISBN: 978-0-692-85368-9

Printed in the United States of America.

Unlock Your Success DNA

WINTALITY

BAYLOR BARBEE

We admire the king of the jungle,
We cheer when the gazelle escapes,
But no one prays for the Lion.

For you, the Lion…

Introduction

"Without continual growth and progress, such words as improvement, achievement, and success have no meaning."
– Benjamin Franklin

A lion on the plains of the Serengeti has her mind made up. In the vast herd of zebras, gazelle, bison, and other wildlife, the lioness has her sights set on one particular animal. She is so keenly focused on her target that the outside world and all other distractions cease to exist.

Slowly, she inches closer toward her prey, mirroring the movements of her target. When the prey looks up, she pauses; when the prey relaxes, she stealthily advances. The lioness knows her entire pride depends on her executing her job, and experience has taught her that timing is critical. If she pounces too early, the target will flee. If she waits too long, she will be spotted.

She creeps into position, approximately 30 meters away from her target. She is not thinking about the heat of the scorching sun, nor does she think about the fact she has not eaten in almost a week or that she is most definitely dehydrated and fatigued.

No, she knows only one thing matters – catching the prey. She pauses, takes a deep breath, and digs her claws into the ground to ensure a solid grip when she bursts toward the target. She focuses her glare on the precise part of the neck she will grasp when she leaps toward her prey... 3, 2, 1. The lioness springs into action with everything she has for this is Life or Death.

What is Wintality?

When a lion chases its prey, there are no style points or moral victories. It is not always pretty, but the only thing that matters is the result. Wintality (Winning + Mentality) unleashes the instinctual nature to succeed by providing a framework and process to ensure you harness that energy and use it in a manner that brings growth and progress into your life.

Wintality is about results. Consistent results, growing results, regardless of situation or adversity.

Wintality can be summed up with a simple, straightforward formula:

AMBITION + ACTION – EXCUSES = RESULTS

We live in a society that celebrates winners, champions, and successes. The problem with this is we celebrate individual accomplishments and idolize heroes of specific events, without looking at the collective whole of the individual or team. You already have a Wintality. You are a lion possessing the killer instinct and skillset required to catch what you desire.

Wintality is an aggressive pursuit; an unbreakable spirit fueled by ambition.

The primary focus of the book is not just to help you close one deal, become victorious in one event, or improve in one particular facet of life. This is not about spreading yourself thin or wearing numerous hats at once.

Wintality is about awakening the natural instinct inside of you that moves the needle forward, unlocking the DNA that gets desired results. It is about becoming a true winner in all aspects of life so that winning is contagious in your business, your relationships, and all other aspects of your life.

In Greek mythology, King Midas received legendary status for his ability to turn everything he touched into gold. In the same manner, you can have the Midas Touch in everything you do.

Each of us has a driving voice buried deep inside of us that is unaffected by excuses, opinions, or circumstances and yearns to succeed. Wintality does not add layers of new age principles you have to learn, memorize, and master to make any progress. It is quite the opposite.

Michelangelo said it best when asked about one of his great works. "I saw the angel in the marble and carved until I set him free. Every block of stone has a statue inside it, and it is the task of the sculptor to discover it."

Wintality is the toolkit to help you chip away at the great work of art that exists inside you. The good news is that whom you can become and what you can accomplish is already inside of you; the bad news is it takes work to set it free. Your DNA comprises strands of success and accomplishment. All too often, the DNA of success remains buried beneath layers of distractions, the stimulus of doubt and fear, and a general lack of purpose.

Isn't your house much better when it is clean? Have you noticed you never clean your house by adding to it, but subtracting from it what is unnecessary? Together, we will unclutter your life, unlock your process for achievement, and spring you into action toward a triumphant life.

You may think, "This sounds great, but I am so far behind and have so much to catch up before I can even think about looking at my future." We are all busy people, but luckily, you can harness your Wintality in the midst of all you have going on. You can start right now. Not only will you see the ability to win is already inside you, but you can also apply it to what you are doing and execute it in a more efficient and effective manner.

Why Wintality?

Perhaps, you are already a peak performer and wonder what you gain from Wintality, or perhaps, you have never really thought about yourself as a "winner." In either scenario, there are fundamental questions that Wintality will help you to answer. If you have ever asked yourself any of these questions, Wintality is definitely for you.

Question #1 – Are winners born or developed?

Yes, winners are born. The good news is that you are a born winner. Wintality will help bring out the winning qualities that exist inside you so that you may win on an even greater level.

Question #2 – Is there a formula for success?

Yes, there is a formula for success. Rather than a step by step guide, Wintality will teach you the Process of Attainment, (PoA), a framework that will allow you to accomplish anything in life by understanding where you are in the process at any given time. This process, whether knowingly or unknowingly, is utilized throughout history by the masterminds in every walk of life.

By properly acknowledging where you are, you can stay focused on the task at hand and give yourself foresight into the next phase of the attainment process, so you may continually build momentum and progress, without wasting valuable time and energy trying to figure out what to do next.

Question #3 – What are the key qualities that all winners possess?

The approach and styles of winners may be different, but they all share a set of unique qualities. Wintality will divulge those qualities and help you find them in yourself.

Question #4 – How do I turn a dream into a reality?

By providing you with action steps to make solid strides toward the realization of the dream or goal, Wintality will provide a blueprint to transition you from a dreamer to a doer.

Question #5 – How do I know when the time is right to "go for it?"

As is the case with the lion, timing is critical. Wintality will dispel the myth that says you have to go 100% at all times (which wears you out and rarely gets you anywhere worthwhile), instead of helping you understand the importance of going 100% at the RIGHT time to get your desired result.

Question #6 – How do I handle rejection and failure?

Wintality will give you a fresh perspective on the words "failure" and "fear" and teach you the power of the word "NO" as a driving force in your success.

Question #7 – How do winners always stay motivated and happy?

Wintality will look at the grim reality of the mental health aspect of winning at a high level, the depression that often lingers, and how winners operate "from the bottom" and remain effective when they are down.

Question #8 – How do I get to the top and stay there?

The Process of Attainment will help you get to the top, but Wintality also teaches you the importance of understanding change and staying on the forefront of change to ensure you stay on top.

Question #9 – How do I become a leader?

Whether you know it or not, you are a leader. The real question is, "Which way are you leading your following?" Wintality will help you identify who is following you and provide you with the skillset to lead them the correct way.

Question #10 – Am I Winner?

Yes, you are a winner. However, it does not matter what I say; what matters is that you believe it. Wintality will help you find the winner inside of you and drive you to help the world see it.

Wintality will introduce the Process of Attainment, a five-phase approach to accomplishing any objective. After introducing the five phases, Devise, Tries, Surprise, Revise, and Rise, the remainder of the book will go in-depth to each of the phases, so you can reinforce your ambitious instinct and fortify your mind to handle the stress and adversity that comes with being a peak performer.

Are you ready to remove the distractions in your life and sculpt the winner inside you, based on the success DNA you already possess? It's time to unlock your true potential and convert it into explosive action to give you extraordinary results in your life, career, and relationships.

It is time to roar; it is time to leap toward a goal, a dream, and most of all, take hold of a winning life.

Table of Contents

Introduction   3

Chapter 1 - The Process of Attainment   13

DEVISE   27

Chapter 2 - The Psychology of Winners   29
Chapter 3 - Profanities of Success   45
Chapter 4 - Failure, What's that?   59

TRIES   69

Chapter 5 - Preparation is Performance   71
Chapter 6 - Purpose and Definitive Action   81
Chapter 7 - Impeccable Timing   93

SURPRISE   105

Chapter 8 - The Power of No   107
Chapter 9 - Mental Monsters   117

REVISE   129

Chapter 10 - Change is Inevitable   131
Chapter 11 - Responsibility   147

RISE   159

Chapter 12 - Leading the Pack   161
Chapter 13 - Letting Go   171
Chapter 14 - Tao of Wintality   179

About the Author   187

-1-

The Process of Attainment

"Stop setting goals. Goals are pure fantasy unless you have a specific plan to achieve them." – Stephen Covey

Nothing drives me crazier than the beginning of the year when everyone makes his or her New Year's resolutions. "I am going to lose weight," "I am going to take better care of myself and start a business"; we have heard them all. Sadly, the vast majority of people have uttered bold proclamations on January 1st, only to forget them a few weeks later.

I always ask myself, "Why do they abandon those resolutions?" I believe people want to make those changes, and I believe that most can make those changes. I question why someone feels the need to wait until a designated date on a calendar to be the person he or she want to be. As a society, we have bought into the idea of a better life more than the reality of doing what it takes to get that life.

Over the past few years, I have found there is an underlying reason resolutions remain resolutions year after year, goals remain unattained, and dreams remain unrealized. The reason is simple – most people do not know what to do next.

How often in your life have you hit a high point of success or hit rock bottom and asked yourself the dreaded question, "Now what?" It is the inability to answer the "Now what" that keeps us stuck in repetitive cycles. Sadly, anything that stays in the same cycle with no outlet to grow eventually dies.

The Dead Sea

The historic Dead Sea, a large lake between Israel and Jordan, possesses a salt content over eight times that of the ocean. The lake, as its name suggests, is dead. Due to its high salt concentration, no marine life can survive in its waters. The reason the lake is so high in salt is that it has no outlet. It has no river stemming from it. Therefore, its waters go nowhere. The only way water can escape is to evaporate, leaving the salt behind.

In much the same manner, a dream will ultimately die if it cannot grow – if there's no process for it to flow through or follow. Stagnant water becomes infected; dreams become nightmares, and goals not acted upon become regrets.

Fortunately, a process will allow you to reach levels you have only dreamed of and crush any goal you have set. Even better is that you already know it, you just might not know that you do. When you look at this system, The

Process of Attainment, you can reflect on the successes in your life and realize you followed this process. In doing so, you will have more confidence going forward in new ventures. Consciously thinking about the Process of Attainment will allow you to get the most out of all facets of your life.

This five-phase process is simple enough that you can memorize it and apply it if you only read this chapter. The remainder of the book goes into detail about each step, so you can reinforce your knowledge and dig deeper inside of yourself to unlock your maximum potential.

Think about the person in your life that motivates you the most, someone that pushes you to be your best. Perhaps it is a coach, a colleague, a family member, or a friend. Now think about what they do. If you are honest with yourself, it is not that they pour in anything new into you that makes them so valuable. Yea sure, they pass on knowledge and give helpful tips, but the central theme of what they provide is their ability to get out of you the potential they see buried inside you.

Don't you think it is time for you to do that yourself? It is time for you to light your fire, burn with passion, and exceed all of your expectations.

Without further ado.

On second thought, pause for a second. I would do you a disservice if I served up a strategy on a platter and had you believe you could sing Kumbaya as you skip into a fairytale of bliss and happiness. If that is what you were looking for, Wintality is not for you. The majority of the journey to getting what you want is often unpleasant. It is not always pretty, and at times, you will question if you are on the right path. Often, when you question that the most, you are the closest to where you want to be. Adversity is always the doorstep to success. If your purpose is large enough, then the journey will be worth it. If your aim is not high enough and the result is not worth the work, you simply haven't dared to dream greatly.

There are no small dreams inside anyone, only small visions with self-imposed "realities" that prohibit us from seeing what we can become. Once you open the retractable roof or false ceiling that's keeping you from breaking through, your vision will inevitably grow.

If you are ready to embrace the challenges to get the results you are looking for, no matter how pretty or ugly the process is, then let's grab life by the horns and take control of our destinies.

Phase 1 – Devise

It hurts me when I see people with unbridled passion, thirsty to go out in the world and reach the mountain tops, but have no idea how they plan to go about it or even care to have a plan. We have all been there. We get pumped up about an idea, and we are eager to hit the ground running. Often we do. What happens? If you are like me, you waste a whole lot of time and energy only to realize you are exactly where you started.

If you leave your car in park and slam on the gas, what happens? The tires squeal, the engine revs, the RPM's red line, but the car does not move. Did the vehicle work hard? Absolutely. It worked so hard that if you keep doing that, you will destroy the engine in the vehicle.

Do you see the similarities in your life? Your foot is on the gas, and you are burning both ends of the candle, but you do not progress in life. You are not alone. The good news is that can change right now. Just as a car is hard wired to do what it was designed to do when told to do it, your mind and body are wired to do what they are instructed to do.

When a car is shifted into drive, it moves forward. When you turn the steering wheel, the vehicle responds accordingly. The car was engineered to react to the plans and direction of the creator. The makers of the vehicle spent countless hours devising every nuance of the vehicle to ensure it provided every benefit to the driver and could get the driver to its intended destination.

In designing your life, your future will gladly follow the plan you set – as long as you set a plan.

Ask yourself the following questions and be specific in your answers:

- What am I trying to accomplish?
- What am I willing to do to accomplish my goal?
- What foreseeable obstacles stand between me and my goal and how will I conquer them?

- What feeling will I get when I accomplish the task at hand?
- Who will benefit if I reach this goal and how will they benefit?
- In what way will I become a better person when I accomplish this task?

These may seem like simple questions to you. You may not have thought about some. Throughout the years, I have learned that it is not the answer that's hard to produce, but asking ourselves the right questions.

Though we discuss goals, the true goal should be to realize your maximum potential, so you operate at peak performance in all areas of your life. When peak performance becomes your focus, various aspects of life will take care of themselves.

Devise a plan geared toward creating a peak-performing version of yourself and create a basic roadmap of how you will become that person. Don't worry about the details; just picture a maximum you. Is it a person with a solid family, a booming career, or perhaps someone that's a pillar of hope for those around you? There are no wrong answers; what is important is who YOU want to be, not what others want you to be.

Don't overthink it; just write. It is already inside you. The answers need not be found; they need to be freed.

Phase 2 – Tries

Faith without works is dead. Whether that is faith in a higher power, faith in yourself, or faith in what you are doing, the result is death if no work follows it. That means you have to do SOMETHING. There are certain fundamental laws of the universe. Day always follows night; the clock always ticks at the same speed, and gravity keeps us on the ground. These laws never change.

You know what else never changes? The mindsets of dreams and goals. Dreams do not dream about you and find you, while you sit there waiting to be scooped off your feet like a princess in a Disney movie. Goals do not grow minds of their own and come searching for you, simply because you write a fancy list of all the things you wish to accomplish. The person you want to become doesn't tire of waiting for you and seek you out instead.

You have to do something. What you do is not nearly as important as the fact you are doing something. Over 85% of businesses fail in their first year. That is an alarming statistic that makes most people apprehensive about starting one. It seems like a high percentage, until you compare it to the number of businesses that fail from those that don't try. One Hundred Percent of all those "business plans" with no action fail. Every one of them. Would you rather have a 15% chance of success or a 0% chance?

Action beats ideas every time. Doers beat "just dreamers" every time. Which are you?

We do not want wasted energy or action, but if you answered the questions honestly when you devised a plan, then you are clearer on the actions you need to take to get to your intended result. Remember, we are not tied to the method or the path; we are tied to the result. The path we take will alter, but the finish line will not. You can have the best plan in the world and follow it to the T, but if you are chasing something worthwhile, something unexpected always happens.

Phase 3 – Surprise

One of the biggest misconceptions of success is that. when you gain momentum and live inside your purpose, things just fall into place. While this may be fundamentally true, momentum puts you in a spotlight and a spotlight attracts all things - not just the good ones.

Why do bug zappers work? Bugs are attracted to the light. Shadows only follow the light, never the darkness.

In grasping that, it should become certain to you that a surprise will always present itself when working toward what you want to be. Something will go wrong. Say this to yourself, "SOMETHING WILL GO WRONG. IT IS JUST A PART OF THE PROCESS."

Do you believe that? Unfortunately, most don't and, therefore, their dreams die. However, you are different. When you look at the Process of Attainment and come to grips with the fact something will happen, it allows you to remain calm in the face of adversity. What will happen or how the surprise comes doesn't matter as much knowing it will come and preparing your mind to face the challenge head on.

Navy SEALS go through "hell week" in their training, almost six days of extreme terrain training with a combined total of fewer than four hours of sleep. The recruits are immersed in the most strenuous circumstances, having to run, swim, crawl through mud, and perform the most grueling exercises on the planet to test their mental toughness and will. Hell week, the third week in the training, eliminates 75% of these elite recruits. Though I do not mean to understate the superior physical and mental condition these elite men and women are in, one of the major keys to surviving hell week is this – be prepared for the unexpected.

I asked a SEAL what the experience of hell week was like, and he responded with three words, "cold and wet." These brave men and women, no doubt, face life or death surprise obstacles in the defending of our freedoms we could never fathom. They are trained to remain calm, expect adversity, and push through regardless.

The surprise in your life most likely isn't life or death, but you can embrace the same mindset of being prepared, no matter what life throws at you by accepting that unforeseen challenges will come your way. Changing your perspective on surprises will change your likelihood of successful results. Until this point, you might have looked at surprises as dead ends. A change of perspective will allow you to view them simply as walls to be jumped over, walked around, dug underneath, or ran through, but never stopped in front of.

Phase 4 – Revise

Don't you hate that old phrase, "The first step is the hardest?" As achievement-oriented people, we know that is a complete lie. The first step is not the hardest; the step when have faced your greatest adversities and have nothing left – THAT is the hardest step to take.

Life has conditioned us to believe moving forward is the only way to make progress. This could not be further from the truth.

How often were you able to give phenomenal advice to a friend or colleague on a relationship or business idea, but when you faced a similar situation, couldn't find the answer if your life depended on it? How come? Often, it is because you are too close to the situation.

We see evidence of this all the time in athletics. It is always the "armchair quarterback" in his recliner on his 7th beer that shouts at the television about what the team should do. It is always the fan in the cheap seats yelling at the referee for missing a call. The view is a lot different from the sideline. Unfortunately, the life of a Wintality minded go-getter never lives on the sideline.

We are not naïve enough to believe that, by continually walking into a brick wall, the wall will somehow give up and fall or move out of our way. However, we also don't have time to view our life from an outsider's perspective, so what we can we do to move forward?

The answer is simple – step back. We need to change how we view success. Success is not about showing others you are constantly moving forward, but getting to your desired result or state of being. Time is the only common denominator that no one has control of, so we must be sure we maximize our time. Successful people simply utilize their time better by understanding that stepping back to get a clearer picture of a situation is the surest way to save time by correcting the issue and moving forward in an efficient manner.

Is it faster to hammer a square peg into a round hole or to step back and find a round peg to fit in the round hole? Is it faster to walk through a wall or to step back and find the door? In your relationships, is it faster to limp along in a relationship you know is wrong for you and will lead nowhere or to remove yourself and find one that will last? In your business, is it faster to beg a certain type of clientele to buy your product or to re-prospect your clients and find those who are a better fit to buy what you offer?

You have a plan, you have given a solid effort and accepted that something will happen to try to throw you off your path; now you must revise your plan. Remember, the path can change, but never the result. Too often, people change their finish line to something "more realistic", instead of finding a different path to get to the original finish line.

In this phase, the revision may be a small tweak. Perhaps, it might just have been bad timing, and you may now return to the action that got you this far, or you may need to go back and revisit the questions in the devisive stage with the newfound information you have. That is ok. In some areas of your life, you will seem to breeze through the stages, and in other areas, you will bounce up and down the stages. As long as you stick with the process, no matter how often you have to step back or propel forward, you eventually will get to the final stage.

Phase 5 – Rise

All hard work pays off. That does not mean all hard work pays off the first time, but eventually, it always pays off. That is because each attempt gives you experience and knowledge, which you can then apply to the process and will ultimately help you exceed your intended goal.

Think about the last time you put together a puzzle. How often did you think a piece fit and, therefore, tried to force it to fit, but ultimately, gave up on the piece for the time being and, instead, picked a different piece? It was a tedious process in deciding where to start, making your first attempts, switching out pieces, trying out new sections of the board, and little by little, watching the picture come into focus. Break it down - what did you do?

- **Devise** – based on what you were building, you created a plan, most likely by agreeing to work on the border first.

- **Tries** – you arranged the border and went after distinguishing marks in the remainder of the puzzle.
- **Surprise** – a particular section was harder than you thought it would be.
- **Revise** – you worked on another piece of the puzzle and slowly it came together.

You repeated this process until, finally, you reached Phase 5, Rise. Rising is the momentum you get when your finish line comes into focus or when you are on the verge of breaking through the barrier that has held you back. You can see it, you can feel it, it becomes your new reality.

Obviously, you want to accomplish more than putting together puzzles. The point of the illustration is to reinforce in you the belief you already possess and have utilized this process many times since birth. Don't believe me? Give a toddler a puzzle made for his or her age. If you observe closely, you will realize they follow the Process of Attainment. You will also realize all of life's goals are just puzzles with real-time changing pieces.

You have followed this process in every successful area of your life. The remainder of Wintality will help you delve deeper into each of the phases above, so you can continue to chip away at the boulders that weigh you down, unlock the authentic you, and break through to an elite version of yourself that you never knew existed.

WINTALITY ACTION STEP: Recall the largest milestones in your life and write down the phases of the Process of Attainment you went through to achieve them.

DEVISE

"Setting a goal is not the main thing. It is deciding how you will go about achieving it and staying with that plan." – *Tom Landry*

-2-

The Psychology of Winners

"Our environment, the world in which we live and work, is a mirror of our attitudes and expectations."
– Earl Nightingale

I have never been a fan of watching television. With so many things I want to accomplish, I never saw the point in wasting hours a day watching others live their dreams. However, one week out of the year, I stay glued to the TV. That week is Shark Week on the Discovery Channel. If you are not familiar with it, Shark Week is a week devoted to nothing but sharks, with a focus on the Great White Shark. I am obsessed. Not just because they are feared creatures, but I remain obsessed for another reason – Sharks are the epitome of Wintality.

Sharks have been on the earth for hundreds of millions of years, and the Great White has been found to have been on the Earth for at least 16 million years. If that is not a lesson in longevity, I do not know what is. Anytime someone (or something) has been on top for an extended period, there are always lessons you can learn from them.

I asked myself, how have sharks stayed so dominant for all these years, and how can I apply those characteristics to my life?

The interesting quality about Great White sharks is that their entire existence relies on moving forward. Their gills oxygenate their blood by swimming forward through the water. If a shark stops moving forward for a certain period, the shark dies. Imagine if you had a mentality that forced you to move forward at all times? How much further would you be if you did not allow yourself to remain idle? Not that you will have no setbacks, but at the core of who you are, your being needs to have a "move forward, don't sit still" mentality. In sales, they call it ABC (always be closing). Coaches on teams tell their players "go get 'em." Nike's slogan says it best, "Just Do it." They are all saying the same thing – move forward.

How often have you referred to the lead salesman in your office or that friend of yours that always gets things done as a shark? What are you saying? You are saying they go for "the kill," the sale, the opportunity, or whatever the target may be.

Great Whites are, perhaps, the world's most feared predator, meaning they fear nothing in pursuit of what they want. It is fascinating to watch sharks in feeding time. When surrounded by a plethora of potential meals, they remain calm; they look for a specific opportunity. The Sharks are looking for the meal THEY want, not settling for, simply because an option is available. How often have you jumped at a good opportunity and missed out on a great one?

Sharks can remain patient because they are confident in their ability to catch their prey. Their nonchalant, seemingly lackadaisical demeanor results from their belief. When you are confident in who you are, you can focus on attaining what you desire, not just what is available. A shark need not alert everyone that it is a shark to be respected. When you believe in yourself and consistently show results, others will talk for you. Track records never lie. Sharks have a track record of success and you are developing one as well.

The sharks continue to coast through all the potential prey until they find what they want, and when they focus in on the specific prey, they accelerate toward it fearlessly. In the same manner, when you lock in on what you want, it is time to go for it!

A Shark Wintality can set the tone for a winning life. Obviously, you do not live underwater chasing sea lions and seals, so there are a few other characteristics you will need to possess. Again, this is not for those who do anything to win one time; these qualities are exhibited in lifetime winners, those who consistently win in all areas of their life.

Without releasing these qualities inside yourself, you can never reach what you are capable of becoming.

Tenacity

Are you willing to hold on to the idea of a better future or a better you so strongly, with a grip so tight, there is no way that destiny can escape you? Winners in life are the most determined people. Grasp your future so strongly that those who look up to you see it as well.

When I was younger, I received the opportunity to go water skiing for the first time. I knew nothing about water skiing or how it worked. They gave me two simple rules. First, put your feet on the skis and face forward, and second, don't let go of the rope. As you probably guessed, there was more to skiing than that, and quickly after popping up, the skis went a different direction. Though my skis did not want to participate, I stuck to my two rules, most notably the second rule. I did not let go of the rope. Once the waves cleared, and it became evident that I was not skiing, the boat driver stopped the boat. It was only then that they realized they had been dragging me through the lake.

I do not know how much water I inhaled being drug through the waters on that hot summer afternoon, but I know this; winners do not let go of the rope. Winner's don't let go of a dream or an idea that resonates so strongly in their mind they cannot stop thinking about it. This is because winners realize that winning is not always about being the best; sometimes, it is about holding on the longest.

In 1954, a young singer with an edgy style and even edgier wardrobe took the stage at the Grand Ole Opry. With confidence, he sang his heart out to the packed crowd. After his performance, the manager of the legendary performance hall fired him and told him not to quit his day job driving trucks because he'd never make it in the music business. The artist continued performing with his sequined jumpsuits and rock-n-roll style music. The artist, Elvis Presley, would sell about one billion albums worldwide. Not bad for a truck driver, eh?

How can you become more determined?

Focus on your Strengths

Contrary to popular belief, you should spend more time enhancing your strengths than you spend trying to strengthen your weaknesses. Winners realize they will not be great at everything, but they can be the best at something. We all have different gifts and talents; why wouldn't you put those on permanent display? In the same time you could spend trying to become mediocre at the things you are weakest at, you could spend becoming renowned in a talent you are stronger in.

We all enjoy doing things we love more than things we hate, and typically, we love things we are good at. Focus on those.

Don't forget why You Started

Earlier, I asked you why you are trying to accomplish whatever it is you are pursuing. Winners in life do not forget the answer. They keep it in the forefront of their mind as a driving force.

Think about your goal so often and immerse yourself in it so deeply that the thought of it follows you around like a shadow. See it when you are awake and burn it into your eyelids, so you see the objective when you sleep. When you remember that, you won't be easily swayed by distractions or setbacks.

Rely on Yourself

All too often, when I am counseling those who've given up, the excuse they give is something to the effect of being burned out because of others not doing what they said they would do. They are often shocked when I tell them, "Why should they care about your dream and help you when you are willing to quit?"

People will let you down. Not all do so maliciously, but their dream differs from yours; you have to accept that. The more you are willing to walk the road alone toward an objective, the more others will join along and stick around. If life has taught me one thing, it is that people love to support a determined individual set on attaining greatness. Become that person.

Don't let go of the Rope

Never, quit or let go of a dream. Setbacks are not there to keep you from getting to your goal; they're there to see how badly you want it and to keep those that aren't willing to work for it away.

Famous paintings are valuable because they are one of a kind and not everyone can have one. In the same manner, your success will be valuable because others are not willing to do what it takes to join you. Be thankful for your challenges and the difficult path to becoming the person you want to be because those same obstacles you are overcoming will keep others who do not work as hard as you from reaching the heights you will reach.

Clear Cut Expectations

My brother is one of those people you meet one time and just know there's something special about him. I do not say that because he is my brother. I say that because he has a track record of success. As a scholarship football player at Texas Tech University, he rebounded from a broken back and a fully torn Achilles. In a few years, he became one of the highest performing salesman in the country for a luxury brand and now serves in upper management for that nationally recognized company.

His numerous promotions stem from getting his teams to perform well. I asked him, "What do you think is the key to building a winning team?" I expected an answer about leadership, motivation, or good team members – you know, the normal stuff.

His answer surprised me. He succinctly responded with three words, "Clear Cut Expectations." He said sales were easy because he always followed the process his company had set for him and others to succeed. He said he does nothing different; he just has a strict adherence to those systems and processes and ensures that his teams do the same thing.

As a leader of others and of yourself, you too have to stick to the standards you set for yourself. If you deviate an inch, those around you will too. How often have you given yourself a "cheat day" on a diet or an "off week" for a workout, only to give up on your disciplined plan?

Mediocrity lurks around greatness and looks for any opportunity to bring you back down to Earth. You can counter this by establishing what you expect out of others and exactly what you expect out of yourself.

How do you set clear-cut expectations?

Identify precisely what your end goal is

In my seminars and workshops, I often ask people, "By a show of hands, who wants to be successful?" Almost everybody (hey, you cannot get them all) raises their hand. I typically then ask people in rapid fire succession, "What does success mean to you?" Sadly, 9/10 people have no immediate answer or they have an answer so vague it will never become a reality.

One of the main reasons most don't reach the level of success they desire is that they do not know what that level is. What is a success to you? Give yourself specifics. People say, "I want to make more money," but if they make a dollar then, by definition, are they not more successful? Yes, but is that what they meant?

Your mind is a powerful tool and will work to get you to where you tell it to go. Think about it as a life GPS. If you do not put in the exact coordinate of where you want it to go, it will sit there idle and wait – and so will your life.

Use direct and vivid language when setting expectations

If you go to an electronic store and head to the TV section, you cannot help but notice the showroom model. It is always the largest television, with a picture so clear you can see every detail, accompanied with surround sound that immerses you in the experience.

The level of detail in the ultra-high definition makes you desire the TV. Your expectation of yourself or your team must be crystal clear. "Get more sales," is not clear cut. "I need you to sell ten more units than you did last month, and I will check on you at the midway point of the month to see that you are on pace," is a very clear expectation.

"I need to lose weight," is admirable, but not clear. "I need to increase my cardio by 30 minutes a day and decrease my calorie intake by drinking water instead of soda and eating fruit instead of potato chips until I reach my desired weight, 20 pounds below where I currently stand" is very clear. Do you see the difference? When the expectation becomes vivid in your mind, it becomes more desirable and more attainable.

No deviation

You will make mistakes. However, the type of mistakes you make is up to you. Don't make "deviation" mistakes, aka conscious mistakes that take you away from where you say you want to be. If your goal is to stick to a vegetarian diet and eliminate alcohol, don't eat a steak and chase it with a bottle of wine.

Deviation mistakes are intentional. If you are not willing to stay on the path toward what you want to be, then you do not want to be what you claim to want to be. You can often avoid these by avoiding situations that cause you to fall. If you are trying to quit drinking, don't go to a bar. If you are always late to work because you oversleep, go to bed earlier. Simple fixes can go a long way. Put yourself in a position to win, not to fail.

Passion

He was not the biggest athlete on the team; there were those that were faster and those that were stronger, but no one played football with more passion than my former teammate at Baylor University, Josh Bell. Every time he took the field, whether it was at a voluntary practice on an empty turf in the 100-degree summers or in front of 80,000 screaming fans on a fall Saturday, Josh took the field like every play mattered. Not only that, he played every play, time out, or introduction like he was having the time of his life.

He did not just celebrate his great plays; he celebrated everyone's good plays. He is the guy that makes you want to play the game because he looks like he is having so much fun. When the video game companies make animations of celebrations, I am sure they use him as a model.

That is the secret to his success. He loves what he does. Though he outworked teammates and though I am sure he was tired and got frustrated, he never showed it. He loved the game. For most of us, college was the end of our playing careers. Not for Josh.

Josh entered the NFL as an undrafted free agent, made a team, and was released. He made another team, played with the same level of enthusiasm, got injured, and was released. Injuries and being released would stop most people, but do you think it stopped Josh? Absolutely not. Josh, because of his passion and work ethic, signed on with the Green Bay Packers and was an integral part of their Super Bowl Winning team. Yes, Josh is a Super Bowl champion.

That would seem like the highlight, but that is not what makes Josh a winner. The other day, I was scrolling through my news feed online and saw a picture of a face painted, toned athlete celebrating what must have been a fantastic play – guess who it was? Josh. Twelve years after I hung up the cleats, Josh is STILL playing the game he loves. He is still playing with the same passion he was over a decade ago. He has won NFC championships, Super Bowls, CFL Grey Cups (the Canadian Football League equivalent of the Super Bowl), and was selected as an all-star last year.

Passion is about doing what you love all the time, not just when it is convenient and not just when people are watching. What is done in the dark comes to light, and that is not just the bad things. The hard work, the love of what you do, the passion and obsession for the art of what you are aiming for will ring true to the world and will define you as an ultimate winner. Not only that, it will keep you performing at your peak for a length of time far greater than talent alone would get you, and that is what Wintality is about – longevity.

How do you identify your passion?

What is your dream job?

All too often people ask me how to identify their passion. Unfortunately, too many people believe they have no passion. That is, of course, false. Just like your DNA of Success, your passion is buried inside of you waiting to be released.

If you had the opportunity to make a billion dollars a year doing anything, what would it be? The only stipulation is you have to do it every day for the rest of your life. With that stipulation, what would you do that you never tire of?

Would that dream job help people?

Here's a little secret – helping others is the fuel to keep the fire of passion burning inside you.

I always knew I wanted to be on stage. I misguidedly believed a rap career was living my purpose. I was making money, had fans, performed in different cities and moved crowds – all of the things I thought life was about, but inside, I was empty.

I would later learn that the reason I was empty is that being on stage was all about me. I entertained people, but that was it. I was not making an impact in their lives and, therefore, not living my purpose.

Is there a great level of fulfillment?

I stepped back from music years ago because I was empty inside. I made a new goal for my life – be a good person. Plain and simple. I started by being positive online and on social media. That turned into being asked to speak those positive words to elementary schools, youth groups of 5-10 people, and small teams. It was never about money. I enjoyed it. I would perform at over 10-12 elementary schools in a four-day period, posing as a character "Johnny Badd Decision" to give kids a real world example of what NOT to be. It was not for the money. I had the time of my life. I was fueled by every kindergartner that booed Johnny Badd Decision and told me that drugs and bullying were bad.

Over the past seven years, I have not stopped having fun. Every stage, every crowd, and every opportunity fill me up. I get a sense of great fulfillment trying to impact one life a day. They say time flies when having fun, but the reality is that your life improves when having fun and helping others.

I looked up all these years later and realized that boy who wanted to stand on stage in front of people now stands on larger stages with larger crowds. The difference is, I'm making an impact in their lives.

Consistency

Every time I run a marathon, I get off to a great start. I do not know why, but the thrill of competition and the fanfare excites me. My adrenaline pumps and I start fast. Some runners 2-3 times my age start scooting at a pace much slower than my world record caliber start. A marathon is 26.2 miles. My rock star start pace runs out of gas well before that 26.2 miles, and I quickly slow to a near crawl.

I always hated that tortoise and the hare story; you know the old "Slow and steady wins the race," theory. We want to believe the fastest man or the best man wins. However, it is not the truth. The most consistent man wins the race. From about mile 9-13, the consistency shows. As my GPS watch beeps feverously at me to let me know I am far behind my pace, all of those older "scooters," start scooting past me. In droves, they seem to fly by me and off into the distance.

Many beat me by a considerable amount of time. Though they could never come close to my best mile time, I haven't come close to their final time because they focus on one thing – consistency.

Finish at the same pace you start. Life may not be a marathon, but that most consistent person will always win. To make a true change in life, you have to do more of the same. That is right; ironically, change comes from doing more of the same. To lose weight, you must consistently eat right and exercise. Running 30 miles and then eating a tub of ice cream will not get you there. Running one mile a day for a year, while watching your diet will get you there.

Performing great one week at your job and doing nothing the rest of the month will not get you a promotion, but subtle increases each month and consistent effort will get you to the next level.

When you are consistent, you get into solid routines and develop great habits. You do not have to change everything overnight, but simply work on one habit at a time until it becomes engrained in your subconscious, and you no longer must "focus" on it. Repeat that process until your subconscious is filled with nothing but good habits.

How do you become more consistent?

Become a creature of habit

Develop positive routines and stick with them daily. University of Alabama Head Football Coach Nick Saban, whose team consistently win National Championships, said it best, "People have the illusion of choices, but if you want to be great, you have no choices, because it takes what it takes."

Find what works for you and do that. Over time, make small performance tweaks (not major ones) that allow you to improve further. It need not be slow, but steady wins the race. Sounds simple, right? It should be. It is already pre-wired inside of you.

Quit multitasking

Thinking you can do more than one thing at a time is the surest path to failure. Society says you have to be all things to all people, but your destiny disagrees. You do not get to your best result by giving half effort to many things. Consistency comes from doing one thing at a time, for a specified period, all the time.

Schedule it

We make the mistake of believing we can accomplish more in a day than we think we can. How often have you agreed to help a colleague or a friend on a project when you were already overextended? Your time is valuable, and your future depends on your use of your time. As much as possible, schedule your day or your week in advance. After doing so, ask yourself – if I stick to this plan, will I be closer to where I want to be? If the answer is yes, stick with it. If the answer is no – reschedule it.

WINTALITY ACTION STEP: What are my clear cut expectations for myself, and how will I remain consistent about reaching those expectations?

-3-
Profanities of Success

"It is not the mountains ahead to climb that wear you out; it is the pebble in your shoe." – Muhammad Ali

D o you remember the days when your parents would threaten to wash your mouth out with soap if you said a bad word? The thought of those soapy suds being rubbed on your tongue was enough to keep most children on the straight and narrow path. As you got older, profanities of any sort would send you to the principal's office. Many teams and offices have a "cuss jar" at work you must donate money to anytime you slip up.

Regardless of where you grew up, where you went to school, or where you work, we all agree on the standard set of "bad words." Why are they bad? Some are racial or sexist, while others are condescending and demeaning. Words are bad words because they do nothing to bring anyone up, only to degrade them or bring them down.

Though we usually watch our mouths around others, we do not hold ourselves to the same principles our parents and teachers held us to when it comes to our minds. Have you ever stopped to think about how much negative self-talk goes on in your mind? You may think it means nothing because it is "just a thought," but your mind does not forget. Not only does it never forget, it believes whatever you consistently tell it.

If someone gave you a hug and that same person then punches you in the nose, which will you remember more vividly a year later? You might remember the memory of the hug, but you will remember the feeling of the punch. Negative feelings stand out in our minds clearer than positive feelings. The body and mind seek to protect themselves and remain keenly aware of the negative, hurtful situations to prevent being hurt again.

You know the adage; one bad apple spoils the whole bunch. The premise is that a little bit of negative can destroy a whole lot of positive. This is why you can allow absolutely no negativity to penetrate the walls of your mind as it pertains to yourself.

You may falsely believe your mind will forget the negative things you say about yourself. Recent studies into the brain's storage capacity show the brain can store up to 2.5 Petabytes of information. To put it in perspective, if your mind were a computer, it could store about three million hours of high definition video.

You may not actively remember, but every negative thought said to yourself is stored in your mind. What do you think happens after years of "I am not good enough,"

"I feel so stupid," "I look ugly today," "I will never succeed"? You guessed it – your mind believes it and your life shifts toward those thoughts.

The good news is you can change it. It starts by training your mind to recognize those profanities of success so that you can stay consciously aware when they accidentally cross into your mind, so you may delete them. By being aware of these words, you will realize how often you speak poorly to yourself, and then you can replace those words with constructive phrases.

So, what are the profanities of success?

Maybe

Napoleon Hill, the author of the famed book "Think and Grow Rich," responsible for creating over one million millionaires, is a household name to those who read self-help, professional development, or any success literature. The book results from his interviews with the world's wealthiest people at the time to learn what the commonalities were among the world's richest.

Many don't know the backstory behind the book, however. After an interview of steel tycoon Andrew Carnegie, who remains one of the richest people in history, Carnegie gave Hill an opportunity. Carnegie wanted someone to interview the other rich people and find out what the secret formula for success each used. He did not offer Napoleon money, just access to the great minds and travel expenses, and he suggested it would take about 20 years to complete. Yes, two decades! He asked Napoleon if he was up to the task, and 32 seconds later, Hill said yes.

Napoleon served as an adviser to presidents, became wealthy and immortalized for his work, and sold over 100 million books. Here's the secret. Carnegie would later admit he held a stopwatch under his desk and had Napoleon taken over 60 seconds to answer, he would have stripped him of the opportunity. Napoleon Hill is who he is because he made a decision.

How often have you missed an opportunity because of your indecisiveness? We have all struggled with it. The word "maybe," I apologize for the profanity, is often the cause. Think about the times you have said maybe. What were you saying?

You are most likely saying one of a few things.

- I do not want to commit to this because better options may open up.
- The answer is No, but I do not want to hurt your feelings.
- I do not know what I want, so I do not know if I am willing or wanting to do this.

Do you see the problem? Maybe stems from a lack of knowing what you want. Winners know what they want. In knowing that, it's easy to say yes to what moves you toward your goal and no to what doesn't.

Remember earlier when we painted a clear picture of what we wanted? Use that as a litmus test in all scenarios when a decision must be made. If your vision is clear, your answer will be too. People may be hurt that you have to say No to some things, but they will respect you did not waste their time with false hope.

Can't

"I Think I Can. I Think I Can," the little engine said to himself. Other engines were far more powerful and far more capable of pulling the train over the steep mountain, yet they all refused. All of them, except for the tiny little train.

You remember the story in the popular children's book about the little engine that could. That engine had every reason to say "I can't"; he was small, the cargo was heavy, the mountain was big, and the road was winding and unforgiving. There were enough potential excuses to last for days.

Yet, the little engine was not wired to accept "can't" as a possibility. As a result of thinking he could, he did. That same formula applies in all areas of our life – believe you can = you will.

"Can't" is my second most hated word in the human vocabulary because 9 out of 10 times, "can't" is a lie. There are very few things you cannot do, yet the word is everywhere. When people say they can't, they are usually saying they do not want to or are unwilling to put forth the effort needed to get a result.

How often have you told yourself, "I can't save money," "I can't lose weight," "I can't wake up early?" Now be honest with yourself; are those accurate statements of fact or are those excuses?

Rephrase those statements as truths, and you can move past them. "I choose not to be disciplined enough to save money." "I choose not to respect my body, my health, and future by eating bad food and avoiding exercise." "I choose not to start my day in a timely manner by waking up at a time that allows me not to have to rush."

When you rephrase your statements, it has a whole new connotation, doesn't it? Your mind cannot process the word "can't"; therefore, that's how it interprets the can't statements you tell it.

Don't you hate when you type a word and auto-correct repeatedly changes the word over and over because it cannot identify what you are trying to say? Your mind does that with the word can't. It replaces it with "I choose not to" and acts accordingly.

Next time you tell yourself you can't do something, consciously rephrase it in your mind to "I choose not to" and see if you still agree. Be certain you are giving your mind accurate advice on what to believe.

Quit

Do you remember that person who had an opportunity to do something great and then quit before reaching the goal? Yea, no one else does either. History forgets quitters. History remembers and values winners; therefore, "quit" and "win" do not coexist.

In Q&A's and after my speeches, I ask people why they quit certain things. The predominant answer is it was too hard or they felt they could not win. What a terrible reason to quit. If you will walk away from something you love because it was difficult, then one of two things happened:

1) You did not want it bad enough, or
2) You severely undervalue yourself.

Which one is it? I understand that, often, we do not want it as bad as we thought; by now, you should be past that since you now have a crystal clear vision of what you want, but the undervaluing yourself, I will never understand.

The reason most people undervalue themselves is that no one ever informed them of a simple truth - Everyone gets to set their worth. If you have a valuable collectible and a wealthy collector wrote you a blank check and said you can fill in the number for the item, would you write the check for one dollar? Nooo! You would probably see how many zeroes and commas you could fit on a check, would you not?

Your life works the same way. You set the value that the rest of the world will adhere to. This is one of the fundamental strategies used by winners and ultra-successful people – believing in the value of themselves and exuding that value into the world.

Think of a person in your life that you and everyone you know respects highly. Someone whom you would not dare talk badly to or try to disappoint. Why do you respect that person? The answer is because they respect themselves and tolerate nothing less.

You are the common denominator in your life. The only consistent factor is you. You set your worth. If you set a low value for yourself, others will hold you to that because everyone loves a deal. The problem with giving people the "sale" version of yourself is no one wants to pay the full price of your time and worth once he or she has become accustomed to getting it for such a steal.

Take back control of your life. Define your value. This is not just limited to monetary gain. This includes your value as a spouse, an employee, a friend, and as a parent. I am notorious for leaving a meeting should the other party not arrive within five minutes after the meeting was supposed to have started. I do not care who it is; if they have not communicated that they are running behind in a sufficient amount of time before the meeting, I leave.

Have I lost opportunities? I am sure I have. However, those same people always respect that I respect myself and are never late again if given the chance. More often than not, it has created opportunities because my clients know that, if I respect my time that much, then I will respect theirs. Opportunity or not, I place more value on my time than I do any meeting or person that doesn't see the value in my time. I can always get a new client, audience, or opportunity; I cannot ever get more time.

By increasing value or, should I say, recognizing your value, you will learn what you are capable of. No one just walks away from something of value. When you value yourself, value the path you have traveled, and value where you are going, you will not be foolish enough to quit.

Later
(synonymous with "One Day")

I always planned on being better for her, later. I always planned on giving her the time she said she needed, later. I figured, one day, after I conquered the world, we would settle down and be that happy little couple everyone adored, and I would give her that life she wanted.

The only problem is that "one day" never came and all of those Kodak moments I planned to give my college sweetheart later, never came. She had enough of hearing about my "one-day" plans and neglect for "today," and she left.

I do not blame her. Her absence taught me a fundamental truth; tomorrow never comes. We only have today. Winners grasp that concept. How often did you say later to something you planned to get around to and never did? Were you going to start working out but decided to start later? Were you going to start applying yourself harder to your work and stay a little longer each day so you could get that promotion but decided to start later?

What happens when we wait until later? Later becomes now, and we are not prepared for it. The sad thing about "later" is that when it becomes now, it only gives opportunities to those who have always lived in the now because they will value its presence.

Winners know you have to live in the now. Dreaming is good, but action in the now will get you there. Procrastination will get you nothing, except a ticket to watch life pass you by and others to succeed without you.

Why do we say later? Why do we procrastinate? Perhaps, we are not driven because we do not have the same clear vision that causes other profanities, or perhaps, we are fearful and don't want to admit it. Later, mistakes are the worst mistakes because they are preventable. You can always control your effort and timeliness.

Later, mistakes do not catch you by surprise. You know when you are procrastinating. Even if you do not know, someone else will remind you. With my college sweetheart, in hindsight, I vividly remember my brother, my best friends, and her best friends telling me to shape up now or I would lose her. However, when we falsely believe there will always be a "later," life hands us a slice of humble pie.

The quickest way to get to your future destination is to make the most strides now. Which result will give you a better chance at success – giving 100% to each day in the belief that giving your all to each day will give you the best chance for a better tomorrow or sitting around, hoping and wishing something good will happen? It takes no mathematician to realize you get more out of putting 100% in now than you do out of promising to put in 110% later.

There are two people. One puts $1000 in a savings account now and the other pledges to put a million dollars in savings tomorrow, but never does. Who would have more money in a year? Putting a million in tomorrow sounds great, but the action of today always wins.

Hope is a great concept, but as a dear friend always reminds me, hope is not a strategy. A farmer cannot plant seeds and hope they sprout later. He has to water those seeds today and every day until "later" becomes the harvest of today.

Your dreams and goals work in the same manner. The only way to get the tomorrow you want is to eliminate later and replace it with now. Then and only then will you live the future you are aiming for.

Realistic

Drum Roll please on my least favorite word of all time – Realistic. It should be outlawed. I will never comprehend the word, and you should make it a point to uncomprehend it. It has no purpose. "Realistic" is a word others say to you to keep you from attempting what they could not do. I have had no one that was doing something great tell me what was "realistic" for me to do or not do. They help me realize my possibilities.

Think about the last person that told you to be realistic. They probably were not in a position to make that discernment, were they? It is easier for a non-doer to say what isn't possible for you to do than it is for them actually to accomplish something themselves.

Was it realistic for a man to walk on the moon with less technology in human existence than exists in a modern day cell phone? Neil Armstrong seemed to think so.

Was it realistic to speak into a plastic object and your voice travel through miles of copper wire and the listener on the other end hear the exact voice and sentences in order? Alexander Graham Bell seemed to think so.

Is it realistic to think you can open and connect the entire world and give everyone the opportunity to share their story? At over 1.7 Billion users, Mark Zuckerberg and the team at Facebook are a quarter of the way there.

Is it realistic for a man and woman to join and over the course of 9 months have their indivual cells read instructions from their respective DNA's, teach themselves to come together and multiply, resulting in two sets of DNA bercoming one living breathing human being that reflects the mother and father? That doesn't seem very "realistic", yet it happens every day.

Stop telling yourself a goal is unrealistic. Quit putting a ceiling on your success. You were made for more. Realistic is just an excuse you give yourself not to aim for what you want. What would people say if you, as a free person, slapped handcuffs on yourself and walked into a prison and locked yourself inside? They would say you are insane. They would ask why anyone would lock themselves up and take away their freedom?

Why are you doing that? Why are you imprisoning yourself in a jail of "realistic" and allowing the Warden, named Doubt, to tell you what you "can't" do, while you promise yourself that you will "maybe" let yourself out "later," but ultimately give up and "Quit"?

Don't you think it is time to take the shackles off of your mind and talent and free yourself to be something great?

WINTALITY ACTION STEP: Make a list of the ten phrases you most commonly use that include the words "can't, maybe, quit, later, and realistic" and replace them with positive sentences that move you toward your goal.

Keep this list in sight as a reminder to yourself. Replacing the profanities of success with proclamations of success is a sure-fire method for unlocking your success DNA.

-4-
Failure, What's that?

"We can easily forgive a child who is afraid of the dark; the real tragedy of life is when men are afraid of the light."
– Plato

Go to any blockbuster movie based on a book and you will hear a reoccurring theme from those who read the book and saw the movie. Almost every time, the audience says, "The book is better than the movie." You have done it too. You probably looked at the movie characters and thought to yourself, "That is not what they look like." You have a picture in your mind of what it should be.

Growing up, most kids fear the boogie man or the monster under the bed or in the closet or wherever it might lurk. What are they afraid of? The unknown. The unknown, like books, give the mind an opportunity to create a reality.

If we polled a group of 1000 people from around the world and asked them "What is the ultimate failure," would everyone say the same answer? No. Why not? Everyone's life experiences cause them to view failure differently.

Failure is subjective and subjective things can be changed. No one wants to fail. The reason most are scared to fail is that most people do not stop to think about what failure entails. Failure is the villain in a book or the monster under our bed. Because it is unknown, we imagine our absolute worst case scenarios and project them into a word called "failure."

Winners view failure for what it is, just an event. It does not define you as a person; it's simply an event, a point in time.

Failure simply means you did not get the intended result. Walking into the White House does not mean you are the President. Sitting on a plane does not mean you are a pilot, and standing in a garden does not mean you are a flower. In each of these scenarios, where you are does not determine who or what you are.

The same can be said of failure. You might not have had an event or a season of your life go as planned, but that is not who you are; it is just where you are. We all fail at something, yet life goes on. There's not a player in the baseball hall of fame who has never struck out. There is not a billionaire on earth who has never lost money or made a mistake. No matter what you do, the best person in that industry has failed. The more successful you are, the more times you have likely failed. Success is simply making a mountain out of your mistakes for people to look up to, instead of using it as a pyramid to bury yourself under.

In both situations, mistakes add up. The difference in winners and losers depends upon if you stand on top of your mistakes or hide underneath them. Winners can look at a perceived failure and understand why it failed so they can fix it. Losers look at the failure and see doomsday. When your check engine light comes on in your vehicle and you go to a dealership, would you prefer a mechanic that diagnoses the problem or one that just says, "Eh, you will be fine," without even looking at the problem?

We must treat failure the same way. We have to analyze it. It comes in one of two ways.

Experience Failure

Experience failures are the failures where you gave your best. Someone was simply better than you on that day and in that instance. It might have been a job interview or an athletic competition; it does not mean they were better than you; they were just better that day. Remember, failure is not who you are.

Again, you gave your best effort, and in doing so, you know the situation could not have played out any differently. Because of this, you did not fail. That experience now becomes a litmus test to improve your performance and learn. These are not failures; they are teaching tools. These types of "failures" are what turn ordinary men into legends.

A Chocolate Dream

In the late 1800's, a young man named Milton left his job at a printing press to learn the candy trade. He worked for a company for a while and then decided he would start his own business. He quickly learned there was more to business than just making candy and his business failed. He moved from Pennsylvania to Denver to learn a new skill in the candy making business, the production of caramel. With his newfound skill, he moved to New York to sell his caramel candy, yet again, the business failed.

Milton moved back home, where he experimented with different candy recipes and failed again. However, each time, he learned something new. Each time he applied what he learned.

In Pennsylvania, he had some success with his caramels due to the use of fresh milk, which he had access to because of the many cows in Pennsylvania. He soon became fascinated with the German's method of producing chocolate and applied it to his caramels to create chocolate covered caramels.

People enjoyed the chocolate more than the caramels because Milton, through his extensive testing and recipe creations, used a sweet condensed milk, and milk chocolate became popular.

Milton capitalized on every failed venture and recipe until he finally failed his way to success. You may ask yourself, why do I care about Milton? It is because over 100 years later, the world still enjoys Milton Hershey's Hershey bars and all of the milk-chocolate bars that Milton's Hershey company has created since.

Not bad for a failure, huh? You have to be willing to fail forward. Every perceived failure gives you experience that can viewed as more pieces to the puzzle of life. The more you put together, the clearer your picture will become. Fail enough times and the pieces of the puzzle will give you a finished product – the success you have been looking for.

Effort Failure

The odds are always 50/50. You might be a candidate for a new job against other applicants, but if you break it down, there's still a 50% chance of getting the job. You get it, or you do not. I do not play the lottery or Powerball, but despite the printed "odds," you either win or you do not.

By these odds, you can look at the "failing" side and understand that half of it, the experience failures, are not failures. Therefore, in every situation in life, there is only a 25% chance of failure. Aren't those great odds? What if we could eliminate that 25% chance of failure and never fail again? Guess what? We can.

The only failure you will ever truly experience in life comes by way of effort failure. Only you control that, which means you can change it. Effort costs no money, but it always has a cost. When you earn a check in life, you get to decide what you spend it on. Essentially, you get to decide what you get for what you put in. Effort works the same way. If you put in your best effort, life has a tendency to reward you greater than your effort. If you do not put in effort, then you learn the true cost of lack of effort – missed opportunity.

You did not study, so you failed; you did not prepare for the presentation, so you failed; you did not put enough effort into your relationship, so it failed; you did not care about your health or fitness, so you got out of shape and sick. All of those situations could be prevented with effort.

How many of your failures stem from a lack of effort? Most of them, right? You know what you need to do.

By looking at your "failures" and eliminating the effort failures, you can eliminate failure from your life. By doing so, your chances of success increase dramatically. It seems so simple when you break it down, but there must be a reason for the lack of effort, right?

The Ultimate F-Word

Failure stems from the ultimate F-word, Fear.
Fear is everywhere. Fear is so strong and resonates with

the human mind so vividly that it is one of the main marketing tools used by companies. Magazines sell insecurity to young women and pose the fear of "remaining ugly", unless you buy the products they are paid to promote. Airlines and product websites offer flash deals that force you to buy now for fear of missing out.

Fear is powerful; it forces people into action. For so long, we have believed the old saying, "The only thing we have to fear is fear itself." That makes no sense. We have to run an analysis and see if our fear is worth fearing. Easier said than done, right? Well so is tying your shoes, but you still do it; this is no different.

The number one fear in our society is fear of public speaking. Yes, the fear of public speaking ranks slightly above the fear of death. People would rather die than speak publicly. This is shocking, since I view the stage and the microphone as a haven where the only thing that matters in life for that hour is making sure I bring value to the audience's lives.

They fear it. I love it, so what's the difference? We have different perspectives. If I held up a Quarter and asked you to describe the quarter, you would say it is round, silver, and has a picture of George Washington's face on it. That is correct. However, I'd then describe the same coin by saying, it is round, silver, and has an eagle on it. The same coin viewed at the same time, yet we see different things. Who's correct? We both are. What was different? Our perspective. By understanding that fear is a matter of perspective, you can change your perspective.

Think of a fear you have in life and run the fear analysis.

- Will it kill you or cause grave physical harm?
- Why do you fear it?
- What is the worst case scenario that can happen if your fear turns out to be what you thought it would be?
- What would happen if you conquered that fear?
- What would you need to do to change your perspective on your fear to conquer it?

Let's run through those questions with the number one fear in humanity – public speaking. Will being on stage in front of an audience kill you? No, it will not. Why do most fear it? Most fear it because of a false belief that people will not like them or not like what they say. Think about it for a minute; is that worth being "fearful" over, seriously? What's the worst case scenario that could happen? People boo you, heckle you, laugh at you, throw a tomato at you (if you are a comedian), or leave. A Boo or being laughed at never killed anyone.

I have been on stage in front of people and forgot what I was saying more than a handful of times, yet I have never died from it. I have also had people try to heckle me, and I have had a few people leave. In each of those scenarios, the world did not end. I learned it does not matter if not everyone likes my speeches as long as someone does. If you conquered your fear of public speaking how much more confidence would you have? You would be plenty confident. What would you need to do to conquer that fear? You'd probably need to learn your material until you knew it by heart, realize that it did not matter if people did not like it because you were only trying to reach one person, and if you did not accomplish it, there's always another chance down the road.

It sounds silly and simple, but the best things in life often are. You truly can conquer your fear by breaking it down and getting to the root of why you fear it. Most likely, you will find the reason you fear something is not based on anything of real substance, but rather just allowing the illusion of what that fear is to become a monster you run from your entire life.

Slay that dragon, stand up to that imaginary bully, and conquer your fears. By facing those fears, you are eliminating the chance of failure. You owe that to yourself.

WINTALITY ACTION STEP: Think about the thing you fear most. Ask yourself the aforementioned questions on fear and write down a game plan for how you will change your perspective on that fear.

TRIES

"There is nothing impossible to him who will try."
– Alexander the Great

-5-

Preparation is Performance

"It is the little details that are vital. Little things make big things happen." – John Wooden

A few years ago, while sitting on my couch recovering from a bicycle training accident, I was watching the Boston Marathon. A Marathon, how cool, I thought. Without thinking, I immediately tweeted how I would enter the next marathon that came to Dallas. Here's the problem; I later learned the Dallas Marathon was only a few weeks away.

There weren't any 3-week marathon training plans, especially for someone who had done nothing athletic in over a month due to cracked ribs, so I did the next best thing. I researched the mindsets of the great marathon runners, and each talked about how they tackled "the Wall." The Wall, in a marathon, is around mile 19. Around that point, the marathoner's body becomes depleted of glycogen, a carbohydrate source that fuels the muscles, and the race then becomes about heart and willpower.

Pretty simple, I thought. I will focus on the wall and then power through the last 7.2 miles after I hit it. What the great marathoners failed to mention is that the Mile 19 Wall comes to those who are prepared for the 26.2 miles. If you are not prepared, your wall comes earlier.

The most I had ever run before the marathon was 13.1 miles. I had an "It is just a half marathon and back," mentality. However, the reality is much different. I learned a valuable lesson; you will never outperform your preparation.

As I trudged along, I reached mile 13, and The Wall hit me. My body cramped, I felt like I was going to die, and everything hurt. It caught me by surprise because I thought this feeling would not come until miles later. However, should it have been a surprise?

Your performance results directly from your training. How you prepare is how you play. Let go of the myth you can give partial effort and expect full results. The adage, "Practice makes perfect," is false. Merely practicing does not make you better; max effort practice causes you to improve. You cannot just show up to practice and expect your attendance to get you results any more than you could expect to get a promotion just by showing up to the office or getting an A by just turning in a paper.

The Great Wall

The Great Wall of China is a marvel. Spanning over 5500 miles, the wall has served as a border to prevent an invasion of China for over 2000 years. To put it in perspective, from east to west coast in the United States is only 2800 miles. Therefore, the Great Wall could stretch from coast to coast and almost all the way back again. It could stretch from the tip of Maine all the way to the furthest end of Hawaii, with 400 miles of wall to spare.

It would take a plane flying at 500mph 11 hours to go from end to end of that wall. Remember this was built in the days before any planes, cranes, or anything that even resembles modern technology. How was the Great Wall built through the mountains and valleys and winding paths it follows? A brick at a time.

The Great Wall of China is proof that big things are a direct result of several small actions. The little things ARE the big results. By laying one brick at a time, an enormous wall was built. Whether a mile or a marathon, you get to the finish line the same way, a step at a time.

A multi-millionaire once told me that making a million dollars is simple. Find out how to make one dollar and do that one million times. The logic was sound. By that philosophy, anyone could be a millionaire. Those little dollars add up to big money.

Any goal, no matter how large it seems, is reached by taking one small action at a time. Focusing on the small actions will give you a result often far greater than the intended result. The question is, are you willing to prepare for that big result? Are you willing to perform the small tasks consistently to enjoy the accolades of the big result?

Time and time again, you see accolades and success stripped from those who were not prepared to handle it. They were not prepared because they did not do the small things to prove they could handle the performance demands of the result.

There is an alarming statistic from a study by the National Endowment for Financial Education that revealed over 70% of all large windfall lottery winners end up broke in a few years. Why is this? They did not prepare themselves to handle that wealth. They did not go through earning such massive wealth and, as a result, did not know how to handle it and went broke.

You may have a boss given his position by being a family member or best friend of someone in upper management though he or she was unqualified for the job. If you stuck around long enough, what happens? They cannot handle the responsibility and stress of the job because they did not do the work to perform well in that role.

Some athletes cheat and gain short-term success, whether it be medals or trophies, only to be publicly shamed, humiliated, banned, and stripped of titles later. They may have been capable of winning on their own, but ultimately settled on using performance enhancing drugs or breaking the rules, instead of preparing to perform at their peak.

Taking short cuts gets your success cut short. You lose it as quickly as you gain it. You should value the hard work and preparation that goes into building something lasting. Every brick you lay on the path to your dream is a solid foundation you are setting to prepare to withstand the test of time and enjoy the height of your success. A step at a time, a day at a time, and a focused effort on each small task is a surefire way to great results.

We all have the will to win, or so we say. Very few have the will to practice or the will to prepare. That is the difference in winners and losers; a Wintality is embracing the will to prepare because you understand results stem directly from that preparation.

Preparation through Visualization

Muhammad Ali said, "I am the greatest. I said that before I knew was." Every day, he imagined the fights, the championship, the belt being placed around his waist, the feeling of being a champion. Tiger Woods visualized that tee shot, the lay of the green, the approach to his putt, and the ball going into the cup on a near impossible shot. Steve Jobs said he always saw what the Macintosh could be; he just had to create it so the world could see it.

The great athletes and great minds of the world all use visualization. Steve Jobs was notorious for his meticulous and endless rehearsal hours spent fine-tuning his product launch speeches.

This is largely because research backs the notion that the brain cannot tell the difference between real and imagined thoughts. How often have you woken up with your heart racing, drenched in sweat from a bad dream? It was, no doubt, a dream that your mind created, yet your body and emotions reacted as if it was real. That dream and the mood it put you in follows you throughout the day, does it not? Though you understand it was only a dream, your mind is not so sure.

That is the power of visualization. By practicing, or taking "mental reps," you can trick your brain into helping you perform better than by physical preparation and practice alone. Great athletes perform in clutch situations because it is not the first time they have been in this same situation. They have already hit the shot in their mind, and their mind and body now follow the motions of what they have already done.

Great minds in business see their product as a success in advance; they see the roadmap to success, and as Steve Jobs famously put it, "Just connect the dots" to make it a reality. You have the power to prepare by visualizing the dots of your success, but you have to do so vividly.

The key to this preparation is to use all five senses, not just visual senses. Let's say you are a salesman and you have a big potential client coming to your office. What does that client look like? What is he wearing? What is the ambiance of the lighting in the showroom and how do those lights reflect off the floor? How is your posture as you confidently walk out to greet the client with a firm handshake and a boisterous "Good Morning Jim, how are you?"

What is your sales process like? Visualize each step as you walk the client through the features. Picture his hesitation and objections as you confidently reassure him, just as you have done a thousand times.

What is that feeling inside of you as he signs on the dotted line? What is the texture of the printed check you receive as a commission bonus from the deal? Imagine the smell of the simmering steak in the restaurant as you celebrate an amazing close for your company. Picture cutting into that celebratory ribeye (or vegan option) and savor the taste of it as you enjoy your success.

Do you see how real that made it in your mind? Isn't your mouth watering now at the vivid thought?

You can apply these visualization techniques to any area of your life. By doing so, you are tuning your mind to prepare to succeed. This will allow your physical actions to improve and ultimately your results to show themselves quicker. Spend at least five minutes a day visualizing every aspect of the process of the skill or area of your life you are trying to develop. Do this when you wake up or right before you fall asleep.

Remember, big results are a result of the little steps. There are no such things as giant leaps, only small steps. Picture taking an ax and trying to chop down a giant Sequoia, the largest tree in the world. There's no telling how long it would take you to chop through the 30-foot diameter of the tree. It would take thousands of chops with the sharpest ax. Eventually, no matter how long it takes, the tree would fall.

Is it the last swing of the ax responsible for the tree falling? That one swing of the ax might get the credit, but without the other thousands of swings, the tree would never fall. No swing of the ax was more important than any other; each swing was an integral part of the tree falling.

Whatever you are aiming for in life, keep swinging. The more focus you put on each step, the more quality results you will get. Award winning actor, Will Smith, said you build no wall by trying to build the biggest, baddest, greatest wall ever built. You do not start there. You start by saying I am going to lay this single brick as perfectly as a brick can be laid. You do this every day, and eventually, you have your wall.

Focus on laying a brick at a time in pursuit of your goal, and eventually, you will have Great Wall results.

Don't forget the Discipline

Lying 5500 miles worth of bricks and chopping a tree thousands of times sound great in theory; just as making one dollar, saving it, and repeating the process a million times sounds great, right? Why aren't more people successful, then? Most lack discipline.

Discipline is the common denominator in all long-term success. Winning is simply committing to an established progressive process until it becomes routine. Winners are winners because they realize doing the things you do not like to do consistently puts you in a position to do the things you love to do.

We fear the word discipline because of the connotation it had when we were growing up. Teachers and parents threatened to discipline us for bad behavior or poor grades. What were they doing? They were trying to keep us on the right path. The legal and judicial system discipline those that break laws, with the goal of keeping everyone on the right path. No matter what, you will be disciplined in life. The thing that winners learn is that they can decide who's in charge of the discipline. By disciplining yourself, which means to stay consistently committed to pursuing your cause or goal, you decide your fate.

Would you rather live by the imposed discipline of breaking societal norms to "stay in line" or would you rather discipline yourself in pursuit of what you truly want?

To remain disciplined, you need to create parameters for yourself. Look at your goal and envision the parameters being the lanes on a highway. When driving down the road, you know not to swerve into a barricade or oncoming traffic; you know to stay in your lane. It is easy to stay in your lane because the lanes are clearly marked; there are signs posted to tell you what to do, and there are speed limits and minimums to tell you how fast to go.

Create lanes and parameters for yourself.

You can establish discipline by taking the following steps:

Establish your lanes

What are the parameters you need to set to keep you on the road toward your goal?

Create a barricade to oncoming traffic

Leaving your lane to swerve into oncoming traffic results in wrecks or even worse. Because you understand the severity of the situation, you act accordingly. What is the worst case scenario if you do not stay disciplined in pursuit of your objective? Equate that to a car wreck. Every time you want to swerve, think about the life wreck it will cause.

Keep up with the flow of traffic

Whether it is deadlines you set or repetitions you add, establish the minimum flow of what you need to do to keep up with the pace of where you are trying to get and do not fall below it.

WINTALITY ACTION STEP: Write down one goal for the rest of the week. List the steps you are taking to prepare to accomplish it. Underneath each step, write down one specific small step you can take to improve your performance.

-6-

Purpose and Definitive Action

"Action is the foundational key to all success."
– Pablo Picasso

You have heard it said, "Rome was not built in a day." This is true, but it also wasn't built by just dreaming, wishing, or planning. It was built through action. Too often, we have great plans, great ideas, and big dreams, but do nothing to make them realities.

Anything with good intentions not acted upon will spoil. Milk is good for you, but not if it sits too long. Food is great for you, but not if it sits too long. Hope is great for you, but not if it sits there unacted upon. Dreams not worked toward become nightmares. Goals without action become failures. Opportunity has an expiration date.

Action without direction is equally ineffective. How often have you heard someone say, "I am too busy," "I am always on the go," or "I am grinding or hustling?" We have become accustomed to thinking life is about the hustle and staying busy. Busy doesn't always equal productivity.

The most successful people I know seem to have the most free time. A great friend of mine is a well-known and successful real estate developer, amongst other things. I asked him how he always seemed to be free, and his answer was definitive of purpose. He explained that, in everything he does, whether a meeting or a large-scale goal, he clearly defines what the purpose is and doesn't allow himself or anyone else to get off track of obtaining that objective.

When you have a clear purpose, it becomes easier to take definitive action because you distinctly know what you're working toward. Unfortunately, we have turned purpose into a mystical word sought by all as if finding it will cause all of life to make sense. I am guilty of it myself. Besides excellence, finding purpose was the central theme of my last book.

Purpose brings life into focus and is the primary driver for fulfillment and focused action. However, the purpose is not just relegated to one lifelong mission; you can find purpose in everything.

How often do you mindlessly participate in a meeting or a conversation with no real goal or objective? Could your time not be spent more effectively elsewhere? We have all been part of time-wasting meetings held for the sake of having them but offer no real value to anyone attending. Why do they offer no value? They lack purpose; they lack an objective.

Hamster Wheel

When I was younger, in elementary school, our class had a hamster. Every hour or so, you would hear the squeaking of a metal wheel going around and around. The hamster was getting his exercise. If we finished assignments, we could sit and watch the hamster. I remember thinking, "Doesn't he realize he is not going anywhere?"

He probably didn't realize he was not moving – and neither do we. Most of us, like the hamster, believe if we just work hard enough, good things happen. Hard work pays off, but here's what most of us miss. Hard work leads to results, but not always the results we want.

You can, however, dictate the results. No matter if it's a monetary goal, a client goal, a family goal, or fitness goal, by identifying the purpose behind the intended goal, you set the parameters and drive for the results you desire. In simple terms, you can be happy just hitting the target or you can aim for the bull's eye.

Dart Champions

I hate the quote, "Aim for the moon; even if you miss, you will land amongst the stars." Thought processes like that will hinder your progress in life. Why? Because they are vague and accept a fate different than the one desired. All too often, we miss our goal and blame the goal or the situation. That is the equivalent of throwing a dart and getting mad at the target for not getting in the right position to be hit.

Why do we miss the things we are after so often? The short answer is that we do not know what we want. It is impossible to hit a target we cannot identify. It is impossible to sustain a worthwhile action without definitive purpose. You have to know your objective.

Sixteen-time world darts champion, Phil "The Power" Taylor, is widely recognized as one of the greatest darts players of all time. He says the key to success is simply dedication plus practice, aka consistent action. That may seem elementary, but consistent action has another added benefit – action becomes second nature.

You may have referred to great athletes or great businessman as "naturals." Sure, they may have some genetic gifts, but their "natural" behavior is simply repeated action. When asked what he did to control his breathing and nerves before a shot, Phil responded, "It is just my natural way of throwing. No intentional technique on my part, I have just always thrown that way." Surely, his form has improved over the years, but when you commit to practicing and improving, everything you do will become more "natural."

Ironically, the only "natural" thing about greatness is the consistently disciplined action it takes to get there.

There's a reason great NBA players can make shots with their eyes closed. There's a reason the hot shot in your office can "close that deal in his or her sleep." Greats are great because they are honed in on the target and make sure all of their actions move them closer to their desired result

Everything in your life needs an agenda or motive. Every conversation, every action. I am not suggesting every event needs a hidden agenda or motive; it just needs one. The more stated the agenda, the better for all parties involved. Life can be summed up as a series of small steps that lead you toward the big result. 26 (and additional .2) individual miles make up a marathon. One Million individual dollar bills make you a millionaire; 365 individual days make up an entire year.

I am not suggesting you must become a greed driven, money hungry, success hungry animal. The objective of spending time with a loved one might simply be to spend quality time with them to reinforce your care and adoration of them. Think about how much more effective that time will be if you keep that objective in mind. Won't you go above and beyond if it is on the forefront of your mind versus hoping they realize you care? It is simple, yet effective, and will ensure you get closer to the results you want.

We accomplish by stating clear objectives. Earlier, we painted a clear picture of what we want - consider that the finished masterpiece. You are the artist. Your objectives are the brush strokes. An artist does not waste paint, hoping random colors, brushes, and strokes come together to make a great work. A great artist sees the ending before they begin and simply connects the dots by making sure each brush stroke gets them one stroke closer to the paintings completion.

Every day, meeting, interaction, and event is a brush stroke in the masterpiece of your life. The question is, are you painting your picture or letting others paint on the canvas of your life. If you do not know what you are trying to accomplish, then you probably are allowing others to paint their portrait on your time.

How often do you spend time with people you do not like, doing things you are not interested in? The reason you do so is that you have not found or aren't clear on what your life's picture looks like. When you truly visualize in vivid detail what you want, the action part becomes simpler.

If you know your goal is to drop 20 pounds, then the brush stroke action of "eating" and exercising becomes clearer. Automatically, by knowing your intended large result, you may take small step action, such as more cardio or reducing caloric intake, to inch towards your result.

If your goal is to make top salesman in your company, you can look at what it takes in terms volume or sales revenue and break down the steps needed to hit those marks.

Sounds too simple? Perhaps, you are giving yourself an excuse. Do you realize that small buildings and skyscrapers are made of the same material? What's the difference? One architect had a larger vision.

Do you have a skyscraper vision? What color is the brick? What do the floors look like? What is the reflection off the glass? Remember, we aim for the center of the bull's eye, not just the general vicinity of the target. If you know life will give you the materials you need to build the life you want, why settle for a small one? How do we build a skyscraper dream? We build it a floor at a time. The keyword is we BUILD it - take action.

Hustle + Strategy

A friend of mine always tells me, "Hope is not a strategy." Though it took years for me to grasp, she also helped me to understand that "hustling" without strategy will not get you where you want to go.

You need both hustle and strategy. Without a strategy, you will suffer the hamster wheel fate – you may be in shape from running hard, but you are perpetually running in the same circles. How often have you found yourself burned out, though you are giving your all and feel like you are not getting the results you desire? Hustle is not your problem; you just didn't pair it with a strategy to get to your intended result. Hard work without a solid direction will leave you in the same place.

When I first entered the sport of triathlon, I watched videos of the Ironman World Championships. I loved the idea of sprinting into the water with my goggles and wetsuit and feverishly cutting through the waves towards the transition area to get on my bike. The reality was much different.

See, I had an idea of what I wanted. I was willing to swim hard, but I had no race strategy. Not only that, I had only a vague idea of what I wanted out of the swim portion of the triathlon. I was good in the pool; I could cover the distance easily. However, in a pool, everything is contained. The water is clear, the distance is measured, and there are lines to guide you. There are no waves and you live with the false belief that the pool swim resembles the actual race swim.

Life teaches us lessons when we do not have a clear vision; therefore, we approach our goals with no real strategy. Ideas are like swimming pools; they look good and enjoyable. Real life is like more like the lake or ocean – you had better know where you are going and be able to get there.

See, part of my race "strategy" was to rely on my wetsuit if I got tired. I figured, it is buoyant; I can just float. However, ten minutes before the one-mile swim, the water temperature was declared too hot; therefore, wetsuits were deemed illegal. The organizers of triathlons do this to ensure the triathletes do not overheat. There went my "strategy." Doesn't that seem to happen when we rely on crutches, instead of ourselves?

I hopped in the lake, where you must typically tread water for about five minutes before your heat starts, and everything hit me at once. I realized I could not see the bottom, which means I had no guidelines, waves were already hitting me in the face, and the buoys we had to swim too seemed like they were a million miles away. This situation differed vastly from 25-meter laps in the comfort of my chlorinated training pool.

Plus, when the starting gun sounded, athletes were clawing and fighting for position; I was flailing my arms as hard as I could to keep up. I swam for what seemed like an eternity, but by my watch was only about 3 minutes and realized I had not swam far. Here was the problem; I was just slapping at the water, not moving productively through it.

Eventually, I finished the race but later asked some pros that were at the race for some swim tips. What the pros do differently is that they set their sights on the first buoy and then trust their training and form to keep them in line and head toward the goal. I would then learn that, though it seems like the great swimmers are swinging their arms fast, the reality is their swim strokes are more about efficiency than speed.

Great swimmers, like great track runners, get the most out of each stroke or stride. World Champion Usain Bolt, who owns the world record in the 100m dash, takes an average of five fewer steps per 100m than his closest competitors. A large part of his success is the ability to get more out of each stride than his competition. His start is not the best, but when he gets in stride, he separates himself from the pack by his stride length, not by the amount of strides. His numerous records and world titles prove it is not the number of attempts or strokes in anything; it is the quality and effectiveness of each attempt.

Be sure every stride in your life is moving you closer to your goal. Be sure you are not just "slapping at the water" like I did, but rather swimming toward your destination.

How do we accomplish this hustle + strategy?

Know where you're headed

Great sprinters do not look at the finish line in the 100m dash until about halfway through the race. The reason is that they already know where they are going. When you know where you're headed, you can focus on the step in front of you, not the direction you need to go.

Rely on yourself

People are great, tools are great, but the only consistent asset you have is you and your effort. Don't have a "wetsuit approach," believing someone or something else will save you or hold you up; you have to be willing to put in the work so you can depend on yourself.

Stay true to your form

Great businessmen and leaders stick to the same process. Great athletes rely on their fundamentals. Practice your process over and over until it becomes second nature. When it becomes natural to you, you'll perform well, regardless of if you're in the pools or oceans of life. Become a product of your preparation.

Get the most out of each stride

Don't try to take short cuts, but ask yourself, "Am I making the most effective movement with my action toward achieving my desired result?" As you improve, you should take fewer steps. There's a reason they say the first million is the hardest; successful people learn to take more effective action in accumulating more wealth. Start

You cannot just plan and hope forever; do something today that will get you a step closer to your goal.

WINTALITY ACTION STEP: List the areas of your life that aren't progressing. Write down what you will do to make more effective steps toward advancing each.

-7-
Impeccable Timing

"You do not have to swing hard to hit a home run. If you got the timing, it'll go." – Yogi Bera

Recently, I was consulting a client on her business plan and strategy. She wanted to pitch her clothing line to a well-respected company that works with some of the hottest brands in fashion. There was one problem. Her company was not ready for that pitch. I knew it and she knew it. She had no product, plan, or any track record of success. I expressed my concern and how I felt she needed to shape her brand, establish a voice, and grow before such a pitch, and she responded with the dreaded, "The worst they can say is NO, right?"

NOOOO. That is not the worst they can say. I admired her willingness to accept a No, but was displeased with her lack of vision and work to provide herself a chance at a potential yes. Her timing was bad. It was not just the fact she would receive a no, I explained, but that her lack of preparation and horrible timing might damage any future chance with that brand because they may eternally view her company as the ill-prepared brand that wasted their time.

When you hear "There's never a second chance to make a first impression," what is being said is, "Make sure you make the impression at the right time." Have you ever tried to have a serious talk with a boss or colleague, while they are busy with several other projects? It never ends well. Have you taken a vacation when swamped at work and spend the entire vacation on your phone and laptop? Did you get to enjoy the vacation?

Perhaps, it is not the vacation, the idea, or the conversation that's bad; it's the timing. There's a misconception that successful people give 110% all the time. That is false. Successful people simply know when to give 100%. I am not suggesting they are lazy or don't work hard. They stay constantly engaged, prepared, and ready. The difference is that, by knowing what they want and why they want it, they know when to give their max effort and what to give that max effort on.

NASCAR Lessons

I used to laugh at the sport of NASCAR racing. How hard could it be to keep the pedal to the metal and turn left for 500 miles? It seems like anyone could do it, right? I naively believed that, until I looked into the actual strategy of NASCAR racing. Racing, like life, is a matter of knowing when to accelerate.

If a driver drove max speed from the starting line they would get a great lead; the problem is the engine would not hold up for the duration of the race and would cause a blowout. If the driver gave 100%, he or she wouldn't finish the race. The driver knows there are factors, such as tire tread, gasoline consumption, drafting, and positioning that dictate when the driver should make a progressive move.

The drivers work with their teams to stay competitive, but reserve max speed and power for the correct times. They understand the race is long, and being in a position to finish strong is more important than just being in the "lead" towards the end. Pit crews and spotters work with the driver at each pit stop to replenish and repair the parts of the vehicle that will give the driver the best chance to get a faster time – not based on the driver mashing the gas pedal, but based on the timing of the race and where the driver is in relation to the field of drivers and how many laps are left.

If the driver guns it too early or spends too much energy trying to pass drivers, they risk running out of fuel. If they conserve too much energy, they may be too far back to make a move toward the front of the pack and win the race. Timing is everything.

In the Indy 500 of your life, you have to employ the same techniques. While it is admirable to wake up and give your 100% all of the time, you are burning yourself out. How much more effective would you be if you used your energy and focus when it mattered most, instead of wasting them on meaningless tasks?

In the Tour De France, an annual 2,200 miles, 23-day bicycle race through France and nearby countries, the winners are those that understand the importance of timing. The overall winner is based on the lowest combined time over the 21 stages. Only a fool would think you could pedal your heart out for 2200 miles in three weeks and survive. Winners realize they have strengths and they have weaknesses, and it is better to keep up with the pack (called the peloton) on the weak stages and separate yourself from it on the strong stages. The timing of each is critical.

Some riders know they are better on flat roads, while others may be better on mountains, (climbs). A rider knows there are stages when he needs only to keep up with the peloton, the main group of riders who all get the same time score, and sometimes, he needs to break away from the pack and gain time or make up time on his closest rivals. His actions are based on his strengths and what his competition is doing. By knowing when to stay consistent and knowing when to give max effort, the winners can have enough energy to finish the race strong and exert extra effort if time must be made up or time must be gained due to an upcoming segment that favors the strengths of a competitor.

Are you always on the go, pedaling hard all the time? Are you dragged down by giving focused effort on things you are not good at and consequently being too exhausted to do the things you enjoy?

You have a limited amount of time and energy every day; it is your fuel tank. Let go of the "burn both ends of the candle" myth. If you are working late and working early and everything between, you will burn out. However, by focusing on your objective, you can make better use of your time by doing the things that you're better at and getting better results.

A-list Effort to B-list events

A lion knows that, at most, it has enough energy for 100 meters of full speed sprint; it knows its limitations. It also knows the timing of the jump and timing of the landing are vital to its chances of success. The timing of the chase and the timing and placement of the jump during the attack are life and death to the lion. If the lion used all of it's energy chasing its prey (though the chase is important) and didn't have the energy to leap and catch the prey, the lion would never catch anything.

Situations in your life may not be life or death, but imagine if you treated each as such. If you treated each moment as life or death, would you be more cautious of your resources and limitations? For instance, when you know you have mortgage and bills due, do you waste that money on frivolous things? You do not because you understand your limitations (budget) in that period and what needs to be done to ensure your survival. Though buying the new car, television, or vacation is appealing, you understand you must save your resources (money) to take care of the most important aspects of life first.

The lion knows the chase matters, but the leap and the catch matter most. She knows she has to conserve enough energy to give her 100% during that moment; therefore, she understands that position and relation to the target is vital before she begins her attack.

Like the NASCAR driver and lion, you need to know what's important, unimportant, and vital and give your time and energy accordingly. Don't give A-list effort to B-list events.

Mayweather Mindset

Undefeated boxer, Floyd Mayweather, regarded by many as the pound for pound best boxer of all time, is precisely that – a great boxer. Notice, I did not say he was the most entertaining fighter, but the best boxer. For forty-nine consecutive fights, legions of boxing enthusiasts pile into arenas hoping to see Mayweather lose. He is flashy, he is too arrogant for most, spends money like it will never run out, but in the ring, he is different.

Mayweather has a clear objective – win the fight. He also understands that you do not have to knock out an opponent to win; you just need to connect on more punches than the opponent and win more rounds on the judge's scorecards than your opponent. He does that. He is not flashy in the ring. He dances around; he does not take unnecessary risks or get involved in back and forth fist fights by going toe to toe, trying to knock out his opposition.

He remains calm, waiting for his opponent to make a mistake or miss and then counter punches – perfect timing. Round by round, he dodges his opponent's barrage of attacks and with perfect execution and timing, responds and capitalizes on his opponent's mistakes.

Round after round, the opponent gets increasingly frustrated, takes more chances, and gets hit more by Floyd, while the crowd boos harder at what many consider a, "running from the fight" defensive technique utilized by Mayweather. He famously said, "I am a boxer who believes the object of the sport is to hit and avoid getting hit." Others have tried to emulate his style and try to wait for Mayweather to attack, but he waits them out, and eventually, the opponent advances and makes a mistake. Forty-Nine fights, forty-nine wins.

Despite the distractions and wishes of others for how he should fight, Floyd stays focused on his objective, remaining patient and knowing when to strike. In your life, you cannot change your approach to your goals based on the noise of the crowd or how others say you should fight your fight. Be willing to remain patient, but also to learn what an opportunity looks like so you can capitalize on it when it presents itself.

The worst opportunity is one that has passed. Timing is more critical than effort. When you combine great timing with 100% focused effort, you get the knockout in life you are after.

The Value of Time

The importance of giving 100% at the right time and the importance of identifying the right time are two valuable skills in harnessing the power of impeccable timing, but there is a final element. Many know a good opportunity and many know how to give their all, but not everyone understands the value of their time.

It's said that the famous artist and sculptor, Michelangelo, once sat by the lake enjoying his afternoon. Rising in popularity and fame, a young girl and her mother approached the artist and asked if he would draw a picture of the young girl. He agreed and quickly sketched a drawing of the girl. As he handed the drawing to the mother, he told her the fee, which seemed outrageously high to the mother. She said, "Why so much? It only took you a few minutes." Michelangelo replied, "You are not paying for these few minutes. You are paying for all the years of practice it took me to get this good."

Michelangelo knew the value of time. Let me rephrase; he mastered the value of time. So much that he compounded it with interest, much like money, and charged accordingly. In his career, he created over 40 sculptures, wrote over 300 poems, and painted and sketched numerous works. These were no small feats. The statue of David, the tomb of Julius II, and the painting of the Sistine Chapel are each lifetime achievements.

How was he able to accomplish so much in his lifetime? He gave all of his time to his work. He never married, had few friends, and loved his work. He studied the greats before him, studied the techniques of master stonecutters, and spent all of his days creating works. Everything he did tied back to what he loved. He wasted no time. Michelangelo was such an avid learner due to the positive effect it had on his art that, right before his death at the age of 89, he regretted dying because he was "just learning the alphabet of his profession."

Here is a legendary sculptor and artist who maximized his time and made numerous priceless pieces, and after that, he wished for more time because he felt he was just getting started.

If legends recognize the value of time and desire more of it, there must be something to it. Your time is the most valuable asset you have. Since time is the only thing you cannot give yourself more of, perhaps, it is the only true asset.

When you run low on money, you value it more. When you're about to lose a relationship, you value it more. When you are about to lose a job you like, you value it more. We value things that flee us. But why? The first dollar you spent is the same dollar as the last one. The relationship you did not put your all into is the one with the same person you first fell in love with. The job you slacked on was the same one you prayed and wished for initially.

How many situations in your life would you do all over again if you could? What we are saying is, what events in your life would you "maximize your time spent" on if you had the opportunity?

What's stopping you from doing that now? We always talk about the "good ole days," but we are just recalling the days we maximized. Eventually, today will be one of the good ole days you reminisce on. Make it worth missing.

Just as your actions dictate how people may treat you, your use of time determines its value. If you are always available and can be there for anyone at any time, you do not value your own time. Michelangelo squeezed every ounce of time into his work, and he still wanted more.

You must possess a "me first" mentality for your time. You are the only one with your personal, limited amount of time to accomplish what you are seeking to accomplish. You may think, "It is selfish to put myself first," but think of what others are doing when they ask for help – they are asking you to help them complete their mission or objective. Even worse, not everyone has a vision, so they are selfishly asking you to waste time helping them waste time.

Think about it.

When you become selfish with your time, a funny thing happens. Those wasting your time get mad you are not wasting it with them and leave. Those that respect you will see your vision and drive and become even more respectful of your time, allowing you to accomplish more together.

As a result of being more productive and efficient with your time, you have more of it to help others. Therefore, the way to help the largest number of people that matter is to become more selfish with your time.

How do you master time?

What is most important to you?

What are A-list priorities and what are B-list? By understanding what is important to you, you can allocate more time or conserve energy to give 100% effort to those people, events, and tasks.

Where are you wasting fuel?

Make a list of all the places you are wasting time or effort for meaningless or depreciating tasks. If it is not moving you closer to your goal, it needs to be removed from your schedule.

Identify opportunity

We miss opportunities because we do not know what they look like. Just as Mayweather knows that a drop of the gloves or a wild punch thrown by an opponent is an opportunity for him to attack, you need to understand what the opportunity you are looking for looks like.

Be prepared to capitalize

Earlier, we talked about the importance of preparation. Prepare yourself to respond to the opportunity and strike with all you have got when that opportunity presents it-self.

Get greedy with your time

Not everyone deserves your time, but you do. Instead of looking at your schedule merely by the hours, look at the time and energy required and make sure A-list priorities get your best effort and attention.

WINTALITY ACTION STEP: Make a list of events you spend more than half an hour on per day that don't move you forward. Eliminate them for a week and replace them with productive opportunities.

SURPRISE

"Sometimes adversity is what you need to face in order to become successful." – Zig Ziglar

-8-

The Power of No

"But man is not made for defeat. A man can be destroyed but not defeated." – Ernest Hemingway

In the most luxurious parts of the world, from Dubai to Beverly Hills, Monaco to Shanghai, Ferraris and Lamborghinis grace the entrances of the finest establishments. Who would have thought a simple "no" would create such a great rivalry?

Ferruccio Lamborghini was always fascinated with mechanics. After serving in World War II, he saw a need for agriculture machinery and built a successful business repurposing military vehicles into tractors.

With the success of his tractors, he purchased his first Ferrari, a sign of success in Italy. While he enjoyed the vehicle, his mechanical mind noticed all of the things he did not like about the car. First, it was too loud. Second, the clutch and other parts were not quality and often broke down. He did not like how the car handled compared to some of the other supercars he had purchased and relayed his suggestions to Ferrari.

He met with Enzo Ferrari, the founder of Ferrari, and offered his suggestions and design notes on how the line could be improved. The prideful Enzo, not wanting to hear feedback from a tractor maker, told him "NO," and suggested he stick to making tractors.

The diss from Enzo stirred a fire in Ferruccio, and only four months later, he debuted the Lamborghini 350 GTV. The rest is history.

Could Ferruccio have created the Lamborghini without the NO from Ferrari? Most likely. He was more than capable of producing the vehicle, as he took it from concept to completion in only a third of a year. Sometimes, it's not about the ability to do something that drives us; it's an event or word that awakens the power, the thought, or the idea inside us and launches us into action.

The word No has been a primary driver in many of history's most successful people. Too often, we fear the word NO or allow the word NO to cause us to give up on our path toward our objectives.

We have to ask ourselves, "Why do we allow two letters to dictate our future?" We allow NO to reign over us, because many operate on a false belief that NO is definitive. Remember, it is just an arrangement of two letters; it is not a brick wall or a prison. It is not the end of the road; it's only a speed bump or a temporary detour if you allow it to be.

What if we reframed the word NO and saw it as a source of fuel, a source of strength? Aren't you constantly hearing the word NO? If we can reframe how we view it, then we will have a plentiful supply of drive to reach our objectives in life.

Pac-Man Power

You have, no doubt, played the classic arcade game, Pac-Man. In the game, you control Pac-Man and race around the map eating little dots while running from the Ghosts who chase you around. You remember the feeling of running from the ghosts as they closed in on you. If you remember the game, then you also know that, in the corners of the level, there are four large glowing dots. If you eat the large dots, everything changes. Suddenly, the ghosts chasing you must now run as you continually rush around eating everything that used to chase and oppose you.

What changed? Pac-Man was the same, the ghosts were the same, but because of one action, eating the super dot, the perspective changed and Pac-Man became powerful. If you allow it to be so, the word NO can be that super-dot that turns you into an unstoppable force.

It is all in the perspective you choose to view the word NO through. Is it a dead end or is it fuel? Regardless of what is has meant to you thus far, you can change your belief now. Success is measured by what you do after they tell you No. No great story ever happens without a NO, without a Rejection, or without some extreme adversity. Time and time again, the greats see rejection and a no as merely the doorstep to immense success, while others view No as a dead-bolted locked door.

Jaws of Rejection

This summer, I attended my sister's Master's Degree graduation from Harvard University. The keynote speaker at the commencement was Steven Spielberg, who also received an honorary doctorate from the esteemed university. His message to the large crowd was, "In a world of villains, such as racism and religious hatred, be a hero in real life."

Such a novel idea from a legendary producer who produced some of the most iconic characters in movie history, such as the lovable E.T. and one of the most feared villains – the Great White Shark in the movie JAWS.

Despite the billions of dollars his movies have created, the greater story emerges from Spielberg's use of being told NO and how the rejection shaped him.

The Oscar-winning director was always a fan of film and applied to the University of Southern California's school of Film, Theater, and Television to continue his learning. The only problem was he was rejected due to poor grades. He applied again and was rejected. He applied a third time and again was promptly rejected – NO Steven.

The young director did not take that as a final NO, but merely a small detour toward his goal. He would briefly attend another university before dropping out and directing his movies. A few years later, JAWS, Indiana Jones, and countless other blockbusters were born.

Spielberg was later offered an honorary degree from USC, but would only accept it if the degree was signed by the people who had rejected him originally. He now enjoys a great relationship with the school, guest lecturing, serving on the Board of Trustees, and donating large amounts of money to help the school continue to enhance its cinematic arts program.

What can we learn from Spielberg? He was not the first to be rejected. He could have just as easily been bitter, given up, and become vengeful of the rejection. However, Spielberg chose the Wintality approach.

How can you harness the power of being told No?

Reframe the word

No doesn't mean it will not happen. It simply means that is not the person that can help you get the answer you want; however, the NO can give something much more powerful – belief in yourself. Don't allow the NO to defeat the opportunity; use it to strengthen yourself and allow yourself to become the opportunity.

Every no makes you stronger. Every no is the glowing Dot that allows you to become an unstoppable Pac-Man in pursuit of eating up all life has to offer.

Focus, not rage

Snipers are effective because they stare down the high powered scope to home in on their targets, and the rifle then focuses all its energy into propelling a bullet forward toward the specific target. A shotgun is aimed near the target, but the shells spread and hit everything around it.

Use the power of the word NO in a Sniper-like manner; meaning, use its power and energy to focus on hitting your goal - not hitting the person that told you No. When you allow your emotions to take a shotgun approach to rejection, you may hit your target, but in rage, you may also hit those you care about.

How often have your loved ones been a recipient of your frustration? Focus on the goal, not the person that told you No, and by any means necessary, avoid aiming your frustration at those who are there to help you find a Yes. Your focused effort will fuel you to success, not your blind rage.

Keep it in perspective

Grudges affect no one but you. By holding on to them, you are keeping your hands, heart, and mind full of toxicity. Why pull the plug and then hold on to a hand grenade? Understand that the person that told you NO might have said it for a few reasons. First, they might not have had the power to say yes. Second, they simply might not have the vision you have. The more people that say No means the less number of people you have to thank later. Be thankful.

Have fun with it

Steven Spielberg did not become bitter at the NO. He realized he was not any less talented because someone did not think he was up to par. He was not vindictive. He had fun with it by making the rejecters sign his honorary diploma. He passionately helps the university by serving on its board and jokes he had to buy his way into the school.

You will make it to your goal, regardless of who says no in the process. When you do, thank them for giving you added drive to get to your destination. You will forever learn more about yourself from a No than you ever will from a Yes.

The other Side of No

We associate NO as a negative word that inhibits our growth or pursuit of goals when told to us. We have established the power in turning a No into a source of strength. However, there is another power of NO that will greatly aid your pursuit in life – The power to Say NO.

Too often, we perceive that telling others NO somehow makes us negative or somehow deserving of giving an apology. How often have you said, "No, I am sorry," or "My apologies, I cannot make it"? Get rid of the apology.

Saying "NO" to others is often saying YES to yourself. That is right. A NO to them is a Yes to you. If you are focused on a worthwhile goal and value your time, then you cannot waste it on things that don't move you forward. While it may seem counter-intuitive to say NO to opportunities, it is worth it if you realize that saying Yes to good opportunities prevents you from being in a position to say yes to great opportunities.

Do you want to be good or do you want to be great? The difference in the two is to be so in-tune with what you want that you say NO to people and situations that don't get you to that objective.

If you are focused on a worthwhile cause, why would you consider apologizing for declining time spent not moving toward it? Would you apologize for launching a new business, marrying your sweetheart, or reaching a milestone? Then why would you apologize for the steps it took to get there?

Saying NO is a vital strategy used by the most successful people in the world. They understand that, by saying No, they are opening themselves up to more opportunities, saving themselves more time, and causing themselves fewer headaches. It allows them to focus on their real goal.

Paulo Coelho, the author of "The Alchemist," which is the most translated book in the world by a living author, says, "Be sure that by saying Yes to others, you aren't saying NO to yourself." He realizes that every Yes you say to others might deplete your time, energy, and focus to pursue your initiatives.

I am not suggesting you say NO to every single request in life, but ask yourself what the cost of saying Yes is. How often have you said yes to an event or person that didn't progress your life, nor did it progress the life of those around you?

Instill it in your mind that every Yes is not a positive and every NO is not negative. Learning the proper time to say each will become the difference in your moderate or extreme success.

You may be a people pleaser or someone who hates to let others down. You especially need to understand that, by being afraid to let others down, you are letting yourself down. Remember, you are the only common denominator in your life. Your life's YES will come from your ability to say No.

How do You say No?

Remember your goal

Without a focus on where you want to go or what you want to accomplish, you will aimlessly float through life. By knowing where you want to go, you can decipher if saying yes or no will get you closer to that goal.

Be assertive

Care about your life and future. Become confident in your ability to become that person and say NO with confidence. Those around you may not like it at first, but those that care about your future will eventually respect you for it.

Don't apologize

Greatness does not apologize. So don't apologize for answering in a manner that helps you get closer to your intended destination. You should never be sorry for pursuing a worthwhile purpose.

WINTALITY ACTION STEP: Before you say the word YES, ask yourself – will this get me closer to being whom I wish to become? What is one situation you're facing you know you need to say No to? Say No.

-9-

Mental Monsters

"Monsters are real, and ghosts are real too. They live inside us, and sometimes, they win." – Stephen King

Mary Shelley's classic book Frankenstein tells the story of a man obsessed with finding the secret of life. For months on end, the scientist, Victor Frankenstein, attempted to create life by assembling old body parts. One frightful night, the monster, the very thing he had worked tirelessly to create, came to life - Victor was horrified at what he saw.

Frankenstein would spend the majority of his life avoiding his monster, but deep down, he knew the monster was always lurking. By trying to elude his creation, the monster extracted revenge on everything around him, loved ones, friends, and family.

By the time he finally tried to face his monster, it was too late. By then, the monster was too strong, too smart, and outlived Victor Frankenstein.

We may not physically try to create new beings, but inside each one of us lives a monster, and either we conquer it or it will consume us. The monsters go by many names, including self-doubt, perfection, procrastination, fear of failure, greed, and narcissism, to name a few. Others remain nameless, yet burn inside of us.

The more highly successful the person, the higher the likelihood of a great monster inside. The higher the ascent, the higher the stakes. Some of the most renowned people in history suffered from larger monsters – mental illness, bi-polar disorder, manic depression, and extreme rage.

If you're driven, you might have even given yours a name. The philosopher Socrates extensively documented his conversations with his internal monster, whom he named Daimon. In times of extreme stress and pressure, you no doubt feel your monster aching to take control.

Embrace it.

Let's get rid of the pretense you have to hide mental adversities. Like Frankenstein, running from them or trying to bury them will ultimately cause you to lose the battle to your mind. We are not making light of the fact that some need clinical help and medication, but for the vast majority of us, these monsters become uncontrollable, simply because we try to hide them or hide from them.

Though rarely talked about, this is a common trait in success-minded individuals. The difference in those that succeed and those who lose the battle to their mental monsters is whether you use the monster to propel you forward or you allow them to roam freely and destroy everything around you.

This is especially true in creatives. These struggles are not limited to just artists or musicians, but often CEO's and other people in business who create businesses, marketing plans, and those that try to shape the course of their companies, societies, or destinies.

This struggle is tied largely to the fact that driven individuals are passionate about what they do. They love what they do so much they feel a genuine connection to their actions and course of life. By being 100% emotionally invested in their lives, they feel everything. That allows them to feel the bliss from the top of the mountain when things go well and feel the disparity and valleys when things do not go as planned.

Embrace it.

The key word is to embrace, not succumb to it. Before you can make any real progress, understand this monster is a part of who you are. You should never be ashamed of who you are. Just as some may have physical, socioeconomic, or other parameters they must function inside of, your monster is a part of you.

In embracing the monster that is a part of your being, your DNA, you employ it as if it were your employee. Make it work for you not against you.

How do you employ the monsters in your mind?

Be honest with yourself

Get rid of the "This does not pertain to me; I'm not crazy" mindset. Realize, often, the monster in your mind is doing its best to protect you, no matter how it may come across to the outside world. To deny it is existence is to deny it's power and to lose its assistance in your life.

Name your monster

As with fear and failure, we must first name the monster. Do you struggle with depression, procrastination, feeling of lack of worth? We cannot address an issue we cannot properly identify. If it helps you, give the mental monster a real name. Not a name that society gives it, but a name that allows you to identify properly and relate to it.

If I said the name of someone close to you, you could envision their characteristics. You'd be able to describe their looks, the personality, their mannerisms. You know what excites them and what hurts them.

In the same fashion, don't just name your monster; identify its characteristics. By not learning the difference in your being and the monster inside of you, you will make the costly mistake of tying any negative attribute to yourself and continue speaking poorly to yourself.

When the check engine light comes on in your vehicle, you don't destroy the whole car; you address the part of the vehicle that's broken. The one non-cooperative or broken piece is not representative of the entire vehicle. In the same manner, one aspect of you, the monster and its perceived negative traits, is not representative of your entire existence.

Determine the triggers

What causes the monster to awaken? Does it happen when someone threatens your ego or criticizes your work? Perhaps, high-stress times of the month at work or certain environments awaken it.

Analyze your current actions

Write down a list of actions you take when your triggers are activated. Do you have an explosive personality and take it out on loved ones? Do you isolate yourself from the world? Perhaps, you fill yourself with negative self-talk.

Create a job description for the monsters

Before we can make the negative or repressed energy work in our favor, we have to know what we want it to do. For instance, some creatives create their best art or music when depressed. The feeling of vulnerability allows them to express themselves more clearly. Find a "go to task" you can do when you are in a period of facing your monsters. Make sure it is a task conducive to helping you achieve your end goal.

Great leaders create winning teams by utilizing each team member's strengths and putting them in a position to use those strengths to help the team win. Take an unbiased look at the powerful traits your monster possesses. How could those traits be used to help you achieve a goal?

Replace your trigger action

Make a list of your triggers and next to it write the current action you take when the monster awakens. In the next column, write down the Job Description action you will replace your current action with when a trigger is pulled.

Keep this next to you, look at it, memorize it. This will take time. Remember, Wintality is not about instant quick fixes; it's about long-term results. By replacing the harmful action, you take with positive actions, you can ensure you are making progress, even when battling yourself.

The Emotions Battle

How often have you had to apologize by uttering the phrases, "My temper got the best of me," "I lost my cool," or "I over reacted"? Winners are passionate people. While this passion can drive us to succeed, it can also drive us to failure if not controlled.

We always hear the phrase, "It's business; it's not personal." As a winner, you know that when you care, everything is personal. If you are the type to take things personally, GOOD. Just as we discussed in the power of NO, taking slights and events personally can be a source of fuel; however, what you use that fuel for will determine your ascent or descent.

With powerful mindsets often come explosive personalities. Have you ever been quick to snap at someone for something menial or took a permanent action to a temporary problem? We have all done it. We may not mean it or have said or done things in the heat of the moment, but those words and actions, while seemingly innocent to us, have far lasting effects on those they were aimed at.

The Effects of War

Do you realize how powerful your words are?

In August of 1945, to bring a speedy end to World War II, the United States dropped an atomic bomb on the Japanese cities of Hiroshima and Nagasaki, instantly killing about 120,000 people and bringing a decisive end to the War shortly after. However, those were not the only casualties. Historians predict that 80-130,000 people died over the next five years because of the nuclear attack. Though the original blast did not kill them, the after effects did.

You hold that same power with your words and actions. Your lashing out at others may not kill them instantly, but over time, your nuclear words can. They may not kill someone literally, but slowly, radiating words kill the support, love, and willingness to be around you of your loved ones, colleagues, and employees.

When you kill the morale of those around you, you are sabotaging your future. In a speech to the House of Commons, Prime Minister Winston Churchill said it best, "Where there is great power there is a great responsibility. Where there is less power, there is less responsibility, and where there is no power there is no responsibility."

Embrace the fact you have the power to influence others around you. With that, you bear the responsibility of making sure your actions and words do not harm those around you. You may think it is excessive to drop a nuclear bomb, but by realizing that your words hold the same weight in the emotional lives of those around you, be careful of the casualties you will create if you explode.

No One Prays for the Lion

The lion, viewed as King of the Jungle, is viewed by all as a powerful predator. Lions are at the top of the food chain. Somehow, people forget the lion often goes without food for up to a week, while facing the extreme heat of Africa, rival lions, hunters, and other types of adversities. Yes, the Lions have problems, too.

To make matters worse, often, people cheer when the gazelle escapes the lion's grasp. What those applauders fail to realize is the lion is simply doing what it was created to do.

If you're viewed as a leader in your business, your family, or circle of friends, you have probably felt the loneliness of feeling like no one understands you. You are the lion. Co-workers come to you for advice; friends and family members dump their problems on you as if you have all the answers. Others that envy you cheer when a business idea of yours fails or a relationship does not work out.

They forget you are just trying to do what you were created to do, just like them. The only difference is you are at the top of the food chain, and no one prays for the lion. Very few wish Good Luck for the lion because they operate under the pretense that the lion has it all together. You are that lion.

Unfortunately, when you're viewed as being at the "top of your food chain," others forget you are human and face issues, problems, and adversities of your own. They look up to you but fail to realize that, at the top, you have no one to look up to.

Here's the reality – that is just the way it is. Just as the moon goes down when the sun comes up and the seasons follow the same order every year, some things just are what they are. Accept it, but do so by realizing what an honor it is to be at the top. Not that other's around you do not want the best for you, they just haven't reached the levels of success you are destined for and, therefore, don't understand your struggles.

Someone that has never been in your shoes cannot tell you how to walk in them. Applaud yourself for walking in these uncharted waters. Some may want you to fail, but again, it is because they have not walked in your shoes. Others that want you to succeed may not understand your struggles or what you have to face and, therefore, don't know how to help. Some may look up to you as a source of so much strength they literally may not even consider that you have struggles.

This is especially true, because often, we do not share our problems with those who come to us for advice because we want to remain a source of strength for them. We keep a slight veil or mask over our worries and subtly allow those mental monsters to creep in.

Let me ask you a question. If you drove your vehicle all day and didn't refill it with fuel, what would happen? You would run out of gas, and the car would cease to function. If you spent all of the money in your bank account and did not replenish it with a check, what would happen? You could not move forward in life.

How then, do you think you can pour time, energy, resources, and support into others without being refilled and expect to keep moving forward? You are a machine. When you give your all, which you undoubtedly do, without being fueled, you will eventually burn out.

Think of the last few times you have had a serious argument with a loved one, acted out of character, or exploded on a friend or co-worker. Were you in a good mental space when it happened? Probably not. Were you not frustrated or angered by something else? Perhaps, you had too many tasks to complete, too much work to do, or felt like there wasn't enough time in the day. When you looked at the situation in hindsight, you did not understand why you were so upset, did you?

More often than not, our triggers set forth when we are empty. The monsters inside us follow the Monster golden rule, "Kick a man when he is down because he is a lot less likely to get up."

Blackout Dates

We realize that others cannot fill us up. Therefore, we have to be fueled by someone else. Who is that someone? The person in the mirror. Yes, you have to be your source of fuel. The higher you ascend, the more you will have to become your own fueling station. Think about it. How could there be gas stations along a road that hasn't been built yet? Create the refueling station while you create the road. The good news is that it can be done.

To do so, you need to do what many airlines do – establish blackout dates. Blackout dates are dates when passengers may not use their miles, discounts, or other promotions – no free travel, no favors. These blackout dates often occur during busy times of year for travel, such as major holidays. The airlines and other major companies block out these dates to avoid letting their employees off, because they know they will need the man power to handle the rush.

Give yourself blackout dates. If you can, schedule them in advance. These are "I cannot help you" days or "I am currently down for maintenance" days. You need these type of days to get away and refuel. When was the last time you took some "me time?" It might not be a block of days; it might be an hour a week. The amount of time is not important. What's important is that you give yourself long enough and often enough to refill your tank.

You refill your tank by taking the time to do things you love to do, simply because you love to do them. During these blackout dates, you are allowing your mind, emotions, and physical health to be restored, so you may continue to function at a high level for a much longer period. By not allowing yourself to get empty and risk dropping bombs on those around you, your blackout dates work to ensure you continue to move forward in life in a productive and healthy manner for yourself and others – and prevent the monsters from taking the reins and control your life.

WINTALITY ACTION STEP: Write down the largest Monster you face. Give it a real name. Based on the action plan job description you created earlier, give this monster his orders and demand he stays in his lane.

REVISE

"When it is obvious that the goals cannot be reached, don't adjust the goals, adjust the action steps." - Confucius

-10-
Change is Inevitable

"Change is the law of life. And those who look only to the past or present are certain to miss the future."
– John F. Kennedy

In the 80's and 90's, it was almost certain that anyone you met had a Blockbuster Card. Blockbuster was the leader in VHS and DVD rentals. Every weekend at the 9,000+ stores, customers lined up to check out the newest movie and game releases. Blockbuster Video was unstoppable. Blockbuster knew that, and everyone else did too; everyone except for one man, Reed Hastings.

Hastings understood times were changing, even though no one else saw it. He founded a fledgeling company that did what Blockbuster did, only they mailed the dvds to you. Though small, he had a growing and consistent market of people who saw the value of not having to stand in long lines to rent movies, but instead, just opened their mailbox, watched the movie, and then put the DVD in a return envelope and sent it back.

In 2000, Reed Hastings approached Blockbuster with an offer to sell his company and concept to Blockbuster for a mere $50 million. Blockbuster scoffed at the idea and passed on the "opportunity." A decade and a half later, Blockbuster video has around 50 stores remaining, while Reed's on-demand tycoon, Netflix, boasts a demographic of over 75 million subscribers and a market valuation of over $35 billion dollars.

Terms such as "streaming" and "on-demand" are so common that popular apps, such as Netflix and Hulu, are now built into most televisions, entertainment systems, and gaming consoles. The thought of having to leave the house to stand in a line and hope your movie is in stock seems about as laughable as having to rewind your movie in the VCR before you returned it to Blockbuster.

What happened? Yes, Netflix was innovative, and no, there was no way for Blockbuster to predict Netflix would pioneer an entirely new industry and a shift in consumer demand for how they receive content. The real failure for Blockbuster, however, was their resistance to change.

Blockbuster, in all its glory, failed to realize change was inevitable. Merely getting to the top is hard enough; remaining there requires a constant state of evolution. You change and adapt or get left behind.

The same can be said of Kodak, who incorrectly believed customers would always use film for photographs and that anything contrary to film would merely become a small trend. When customers gravitated toward the instant aspects of digital cameras, Kodak was left far behind.

Myspace connected people all over the world. Its failure was believing that merely connecting people was enough. Though, at it's peak, it was worth about $12 billion dollars. Eventually, Myspace failed to realize people did not just want to connect; they wanted options in how they connected. Facebook understood this by offering profiles, messaging, video, groups, and other ways to connect and people fled Myspace by the millions. Myspace sold for a measly $35 million dollars and by the time of this writing, was a non-factor in the world of social networking.

All of these companies made the mistake of believing a superior service, position, or product could withstand the test of time. Never has there been, nor ever will there be, an industry or genre that doesn't evolve. Whether you call it natural selection, evolution, survival of the fittest, or whatever name you put on it, times change, and if you do not, you will cease to exist.

If you are in a high position, this concept may seem offputting, and if you are in a low position, you may have renewed strength and vigor in understanding this law of change. The reality is, whether you are at the top or the bottom, those with a Wintality understand and act on this fundamental principle – Change is always coming; stay ahead of it.

How to stay ahead of the curve

I would not call myself an avid surfer, but every time I am in Hawaii, you will find me out in Waikiki on my surfboard. There's something about the peacefulness of the ocean and the joy of riding a wave that puts me in such a great mood. What's even more important is the life lessons that surfing taught me and how those same lessons can be applied to embracing change and becoming a champion of your cause and not left in the wake of the ever changing waves in your industry.

The first time I surfed it looked self-explanatory. I rented a surfboard and paddled out to where the surfers were. I was positive I was going pro after about 20 minutes. I hired a photographer for an hour to capture action shots of me riding the waves into shore.

Don't we all do this at some point in our lives? We make the mistake of thinking, "This looks easy enough," and launch a business, pursue a goal, or jump in the fire in pursuit of a new objective. What happens? A lot like surfing, you find out quickly there are forces and mechanics of any venture that aren't visible to the naked eye that greatly affect your ability to garner the desired results.

For hours, it seemed like I did what everyone else did. Wait for a wave, paddle as hard as I can, and jump up on the board and hope for the best. I fell off the surfboard every time. My increasing frustration caused me to make erratic attempts and jump on every wave in hopes of just getting on one of them.

In my mind, I had to show everyone how great an athlete I was by conquering the waves. I would later find out that people on the shore were getting a kick out of my epic busts and face plants into the Pacific waters. As I swallowed more salt water, those around me, kids, women, and men of all shapes and sizes seemed to ride the waves with ease. One guy even surfed by me, doing a headstand on his board, while another girl surfed a big wave with her bulldog standing on the front of her board.

I was livid. You have probably been in a familiar position. You are working as hard as you can while someone around you seems to get the results they want without working near as hard you. The harder you work to get to the top, the more you fight the waves, the boss, the institution, or system, the more fatigued and frustrated you become, right?

Too often, we fight ourselves into exhaustion until we have nothing left. Is that person around you simply better? Are they lucky? Perhaps, you are working harder, but the reason people seem to get consistent desired results is that they understand something you do not – The law of the Waves - until now. After spending an entire day without standing up on my board, I swallowed my pride and got a surf instructor for day two. The lessons he taught me are the lessons that peak performers understand and utilize daily.

You can use these steps to stay ahead of the curve in any industry, profession, or facet of life.

Find the right wave

When I was struggling to jump on any and every wave, I had no focus. I assumed all waves were the same. They are all made out of the same substance, coming from the same direction, at about the same speed. I was incorrect. The first thing the instructor taught me was that not every wave is "my wave." For instance, I am bigger than most surfers; I need a wave that can sustain my weight. Not only that, but I have to wait for a wave that is growing, but has not peaked yet, because you do not want to waste time riding a dying wave.

In business, we do that often. We see trends that others are riding. It looks great for them, and we feel we have to take the same action on the same wave. We do not know how long they have been on that wave, what they had to do to get on it, or how much life that wave has left. Appearances are deceiving. We have to wait for our wave. The wave that can carry us, the wave that is growing, based on where we are when we get on it.

The instructor taught me how to look out into the ocean and look for patterns. It made no sense at first, but when I took my focus off of looking to see what wave everyone else was trying to catch, I saw some consistencies. I understood that waves never come alone; they always come in a series of waves. I learned that if I could see the crest (the white head at the top of a wave when the wave starts turning over), then that wave was already on the decline and not my wave.

I understood what the type of wave I needed looked like and felt like. After a while, I paid no attention to the waves that couldn't get me what I needed. In the same vein, you have to understand that waves come and not every one of them are for you. Look for the opportunity based on your needs and its ability to get you there. By the same token, you cannot just sit and stare at change. Eventually, you have to pick a wave. Make a habit of figuring out your needs based on your skill set or position and looking for opportunistic waves with the ability to help you.

Position yourself to succeed

Finding the right wave is just a part of the battle in surfing. Once you decide on the wave you will ride, you have to position yourself correctly to catch it. The instructor taught me how to face the ocean to focus on finding my wave, but once I commit to a wave, he showed me how to pivot quickly so I was facing the direction I wanted to go when the wave got there.

In surfing, you learn quickly that, if you or your surfboard are not in line with where you are trying to go, you will fall. If I am sideways on my board or if I incorrectly guess where the strongest part of the wave will emerge, I miss the opportunity.

Therefore, once I select the wave I will attempt to ride, I have to put myself in a position not only to be in alignment with where I am trying to go, but also to put myself in a situation to capitalize on the strongest part of the wave as it is gaining strength and size.

In your professional life, this same aspect is true. For instance, if you are in sales, after identifying your target buying demographic, you need to locate those prospects when they have an increasing interest. Aside from that, you have to be sure you're armed with the knowledge, product, or service the customer wants so you will not miss that opportunity when you find them.

In leadership, are you positioning your company to ride the trends or changing customer demands by providing solutions that allow you to foresee change and positioning yourself to be on the forefront of it? You must find the wave and then position yourself to capitalize on its strength.

Seek to be in front, not on top

There's a small window of time you have to catch a wave. The greatest secret I learned from my instructor was the difference in my hard work and the seemingly effortless work of other surfers. He told me, "If you wait to get on top of the wave, it is too late. Surfers stay in front of the wave."

When he told me that, time stood still. Much like others, I realized I was fighting to get to the top, believing conquering is about being on top. However, in business, life, and surfing, the top is just a measure of how good you were; leaders and champions sustain their legacies by being in front not on top.

He helped me to understand that, if you truly understand the lifecycle of the wave, then you do not have to second guess the wave. Put yourself in proper position and focus on the feeling of the approaching wave. By doing so, you will know when to paddle. When the opportunity (wave) gets close, you must paddle with everything you have in the direction you want to go. Not looking back, not looking to the side, but gaining speed and trusting the wave to propel you.

Think about it like an on-ramp of a major highway. If you enter the highway at a small rate of speed, you will be rear-ended by the flow of traffic. The speed increase from the auxiliary road to the main road is to give you time to catch up so you can sustain the same level of speed as those already on the highway.

Surfing is no different. You have to feel it. You give your all by kicking your feet and swimming your arms through the water. As you're gaining momentum, you will see the wave through your peripheral vision. Eventually, feel a slight bump behind you as if the wave is saying, "I'm here; it's time to ride." When the opportunity arrives, pop up on your board and ride it.

Work to steer, not to dominate

Great surfers who love the ocean and read the ocean also greatly respect the ocean. See, I thought that being on top of the wave meant domination, but you can't dominate a wave. Waves existed before me and will exist long after I'm gone. Frankly, the waves don't care if I ride them to the shore or if they knock me off my board and hit me with a face full of forceful water.

Industries changes are waves. All industries change; whether you choose to be a part of the change or steamrolled by it is up to you. What I learned is the wave is more than willing and capable of doing the "heavy lifting." It will do the work. If you find the right wave, position yourself correctly, have a period of onboarding to gain momentum, and pop up just ahead of the curve of your industry, then all you have to do is steer.

The reason surfers can do cool tricks and ride back and forth and do handstands is that they never try to be on top of the wave. They do not compete with the wave; they allow the wave to act as their ally. I learned that, if I stay in front of the wave, I do not have to "work hard." I just have to steer correctly to continue toward my destination on the beach.

The reason your co-workers or friends seem to get results without effort is that they have found the wave in their profession or personal life and allow that wave to do the work. It might be a process that their company has in place, it might be a belief system and repeated set of discipline actions they take, but no matter how you look at it, they benefit from the law of the Waves.

By that same token, you can stay ahead of change and spend more of your time steering toward the desired result, instead of spending your time and energy fighting the wave if you will just look for the wave of change and ride the one created for you.

Coffee Bean Results

You can apply the laws of the wave to stay relevant in changing times and avoid the disastrous results of Block-buster and Kodak. If you are similar to me, you probably have an "I want to make it happen, not wait for it to happen," mentality. Though the law of waves will help you in changing climates, the far more impactful action is to become the wave yourself.

All of the power of the wave can be ridden by you or created by you. Your mindset can mastermind the creation of a wave that acts and grows according to your rules and projects forth your mindset. This is the ultimate agent of positive change.

In the Oscar-winning motion picture The Departed, Frank Costello, played by Jack Nicholson, the movie opens with a monologue that epitomizes the creation of a Wave. He said, "I don't want to be a product of my environment. I want my environment to be a product of me."

When your mindset transcends your situation, the result of a situation reflects your mindset. If you remain true to who you are, then the surrounding environment will ultimately adapt to you. However, if you are unsure of who you are, you will become simply a product of whatever you are around and defined by whatever changing identity life gives you.

Do you want to be told who to be and how to be constantly, or do you want to jump in the driver seat of your environment and future? The difference in mindset is evident on a stove top. Take three exact pots of water, set them on a stove, and allow them all to reach their boiling point. Now place a carrot in one pot, an egg in another, and coffee beans in the third pot.

Now, let's look at the qualities of each of these three and identify which one we relate to and which of the three products closest resemble us. A carrot starts strong and hard. An egg starts with a hard shell and a soft interior, and coffee beans start with a strong aroma and rich dark color.

After several minutes in the water, what happens, though? First, you take out the carrot who used to be strong and hard, and suddenly, becomes soggy and soft with nowhere near the strength it once had. Do you know someone like that? Someone who looks strong and confident until they face the adversities and fires in life, and they quickly become weak and a shell of their former selves?

Next, you have the egg who has become hardened by the heat. You may know someone who used to be a great employee or friend with a generous heart, but when they were thrown into the adversities of life, they became hardened, condescending, a "negative Nancy," and saw the worst in every situation.

Most people become either a carrot or an egg when things change. They are not confident in their identity, so they shift their identity with the changing climate.

Then there's the coffee bean. The coffee bean knows what its job is – to make coffee. So, though it's put in the same environment, the same heat, the same adversity as the carrot and egg, it does not change. Instead of losing sight of who it is in the heat, it reminds the situation of who it is. It does not shift to accommodate the boiling the water; it remains strong and shifts the water it's in. It changes its environment.

Because of more heat, it creates stronger coffee. The more pressure applied, the greater the aroma. The water becomes a product of the coffee bean, not the other way around. You have the same opportunity. You face adversities like others do. The difference in having a Wintality and merely existing is that, with a Wintality, you are so strong in your beliefs and self you change the environment around you until that environment becomes what you want it to be.

Not that you should go around and coerce, connive, or bully people into a way of thinking. This coffee bean mindset goes to show that, if you are confident in your beliefs and they are for the right reasons, then you welcome adversity because you know the overall result will be an environment that mirrors your beliefs.

Officer Norman

I have always had a coffee bean mentality, but recently, I met a perfect example of positive change that stems from the coffee bean mentality of one person. This man is Officer Tommy Norman of the North Little Rock Police Department. Officer Tommy Norman is now labeled a "social media star" with millions of followers. He has been on talk shows, thrown out the first pitch at Major League Baseball games, and is adored by legions of celebrities and fans due to his #StayCommitted #CommunityPolicing philosophy he lives by.

If you check out his social media channels, you will see thousands of videos of him on the doorsteps of the communities he serves in a low-income area of Little Rock, Arkansas. In a day and age when many people are weary of police officers, kids and adults of all ages run to Officer Norman with open arms. In the back of his squad car, he carries food, treats, and other items for the members of the community he serves. He seems to know each of them by name.

I had the opportunity to meet with Officer Norman recently, and it was there I understood the magnitude of what one mindset and vision can have on a neighborhood, society, and culture. His personal motto, as per his social media bio's is simply, "110% Committed to Making a Difference in my corner of the world."

Notice it does not say, "My goal is to change the whole world" or anything close, but, total commitment to changing his neighborhood. I asked him, "What makes you care so much about the area you patrol that you spend your work time, and after work, looking and tending to the needs of your community?" He said, "Baylor, this is my home." He showed me the area he patrols, and the high school he went to, the office where he's stationed –in the same area he patrols.

Change to him is not about social media or celebrity endorsements; it is all still new to him. Since he's been on the police force since 1998, he has been doing the same thing. He told me, "People have to know you care. You cannot just say hello one day and leave. You have to show people, day in and day out, that you are committed to serving them and improving their lives."

Because of one man working to help his "little corner of the world," there is now international attention on what he is doing and calls by citizens all over the world for their officers to employ the same methodology.

Why doesn't everyone do it? "Because it takes work. You have to care." When you truly invest in your craft or the people you are serving, your vision will inevitably grow. The change you wish to see will come, but it has to be authentic. Though millions around the world see the videos Officer Norman posts, what most don't see is the impact he is making on his community aside from the videos.

For the few minutes we met, people pulled over into the parking lot where we were at, just to say hello, hug him, or shake his hand. He knew each by name, knew what each was up to, and offered each help with whatever they were dealing with.

All I saw were smiles on the faces of a community that had little regarding money, but they had a sense of peace, knowing there was someone they could trust, someone cared about them, and someone had his or her back.

The consistent actions of one Officer have turned into a worldwide wave of change, simply because Tommy stayed true to his mission of helping his corner of the world. When you stay true to yourself and look to help your environment, you can create the sweet aroma of a better world that others wish to become a part of.

Become a coffee bean and create a wave of change around you.

WINTALITY ACTION STEP: Identify an emerging wave in your professional and personal life. Write down the characteristics of the wave and what you need to do to position yourself to ride it into prolonged success.

-11-
Responsibility

"The price of greatness is responsibility."
– Winston Churchill

Most self-helps books are inundated with steps and processes you need to add to your life to succeed. Wintality is about removing a lot of what you have learned to unlock the winner that's inside you. This is not always accomplished by positive words, affirmations, and a can—do attitude. There's more to it.

I want you to think for a second about your major goals. They could be financial, career, relationship, or other personal goals you have started to focus on during application of the principles in this book. Now, I want to ask you a simple question, and I want you to write down the answers.

What actions would you have to take to GUARANTEE FAILURE in pursuit of those goals?

Yes, you read that correctly. What would you have to do to make sure you did not reach your goals or objectives?

Would you need to show up late? Perhaps, you need to avoid following up with a client or procrastinate on learning the information promptly that will give you an edge on your competition. Maybe you have to ignore your diet plans, avoid the gym, or stay up late, and deprive your body and brain of the sleep it needs to function at peak levels.

Make a list of all of the things you could do to guarantee failure for each of those goals.

Now, look at the list. How many do you actively do? If you are honest with yourself, you probably winced at the realization that a lot of the things you do are actions or inactions that move you away from where you say you want to be. Let's be clear; lack of action is still an action – it is just a choice not to move forward.

Each one of us makes moves that are counter-productive to where we say we want to be. We focus on rowing our boats toward a destination, but half of our ores are rowing us back to where we started. As a result, we just spin in circles.

If you were confident enough to look at your list and think to yourself, "Yikes, what am I doing?" then you are already on the right path toward correcting it. In life, we can make not changes until we take credit for our current situation. We cannot move forward until we take credit for who we are, where we are, and what we have done. Notice I said, take credit. You might be in a position opposite of where you want to be and it might or might not be "your fault." Fault is another of those profanities of success we discussed earlier. The main problem with fault is that it gives you no room to correct a behavior.

Fault is easy to pass on to others. When you were a child in school, you probably played the game "hot potato", where you take a bean bag or hacky sack, and when its hit towards you, quickly try to hit it toward someone else to not let it land by you. The goal of the game is for the hot potato to land by someone else, anyone but you.

Games like this shaped our mindsets to "avoid" perceived bad things and push them away from us quickly. As a result, when a project does not work, or criticism is involved, we seek to hot potato push it on to others, because for it to land on us would mean we lost.

What if you changed that perspective? What if you took credit for your position in life? What if you took ownership of your situation? When you look at it, wouldn't you rather own a hot potato than spend your whole life avoiding them and pushing them on others?

They say one man's trash is another man's treasure, and by that same token, one man's hot potato (problem) is another man's meal. True power rests in the hands of the person who can take what everyone else doesn't want and make use of it.

Case in point, you take the credit for a project gone wrong at your job (whether or not it is your "fault"). Others will probably be happy to pass that blame to you if you will accept it. What are they doing? They are giving away ownership of a situation. No, that project or plan might not have worked, but since it was on you, are you not, by definition, the leader?

In a society that fears blame and criticism, you can stand out by taking responsibility for situations. There will never be a day when there isn't a need for people that will take responsibility for their actions. Much like the power of no, taking responsibility for where you are gives you the power and opportunity to fix it. Why? Because you own it.

Once, when I was in the market for a new vehicle, I had the opportunity to lease or buy. I wanted my windows tinted a certain way, and I wanted the rims and wheels to have a certain look. The dealer explained that it was much cheaper to lease it – but there was a catch. I could change nothing about the car, and I had to be sure I stayed under X number of miles. There were many restrictions and parameters. I could buy the vehicle, and while it cost more, I could own it and do with it as I please.

Fault and Responsibility are the lease and purchase options of life. When we opt to go with fault, no matter whom we point at, we are stuck being forced to comply with the ever-changing rules of society. When we take responsibility, yes the toll is a lot higher, but we can craft the life we want.

So what do you want, fault or responsibility? A life spent avoiding a hot potato or a life spent enjoying the potato? The next time you have the opportunity to take credit for a mistake, do so gladly. In doing so, you are walking into an unclaimed position of leadership and sitting in the driver's seat of your future.

A New Perspective on Fault

You might think to yourself, "Yeah that sounds good, but my situation really isn't my fault." Unfortunately, if you can find no fault in your current situation or adversity, then you can also find no cure or solution. Average people talk about problems; winners find answers. The answer is always inside of the problem, and it usually resides inside the "fault."

How can we reframe "fault" so we can find the answers we are looking for and move into a period of success much quicker? Often, we do not realize we are not accepting responsibility or fault. You may have every intention of taking credit for where you are in life, but subconsciously still pass the blame.

Analyze a situation in your life that you are trying to work through and improve. Now, look at these four types of actions we take when we are unwilling to accept responsibility and allow ourselves to live in a land of fault, preventing ourselves from the progress we deserve.

Deny

"It is not my fault," "It was not me," "I thought you were supposed to do that." All of these phrases do one thing – distance us from the problem. By denying fault, we are distancing ourselves from the truth. This common form of fault avoidance is a sure fire way to remain stagnant in life.

The next time you want to deny something, ask yourself, "How could I look at this situation and make a positive out of taking credit for the current adversity?" In doing so, you will find an opportunity where others think shame exists.

Deflect

Often, we might take partial responsibility for an action, but we don't accept the immensity of the entire problem by using "yea, but" statements. "Yea, but" statements are worse than denials because not only do you bring on the partial responsibility of a situation, you give away the power to take control of the fix. How often have you used a "yea, but?" "YEA I did not close the deal, BUT he was a bad customer." "YEA I am late, BUT traffic was bad." "Yea I want to get in shape, BUT I do not have enough time to work out."

We are all guilty of the "Yea, but" and when you find yourself about to use it, replace them with "Yea, luckily" statements. "Yea, I did not close the deal yet; LUCKILY I have the prospects number, and I am going to call him back after lunch." "Yea I am late; LUCKILY I am going to be able to stay late today and get my work done." "Yea, I want to get in shape; LUCKILY I found a gym by my office where I can work out on my lunch break."

Small changes in your vocabulary create large changes in your results.

Drown

There is a difference between accepting responsibility and drowning yourself in it. Too often, leaders and peak performers have no problem accepting responsibilities. Those that are "team players" also have no problem accepting responsibility because they want to be viewed as a dependable team member. Unfortunately, some become so eager to take the blame that they drown in it.

We are all human and have our limits. When we surround ourselves with nothing but responsibility, we look up, and suddenly, we are trapped. Have you ever taken on so much responsibility, whether by choice or by default, that when you look up, you see nothing but things that are wrong? Suddenly, we panic because, even for us, it seems like too heavy of a load.

The monsters we discussed in a previous chapter feed on this drowning aspect of fault. They tell us, "No one will help you," or even worse; they prevent us from asking for help. I am guilty of it, and I know I am not the only one.

Understand that asking for help is not a sign of weakness; it is a sign of strength. Sometimes, we bite off more than we can chew. When you find yourself overwhelmed and wallowing in the problems you took credit for, ask for help.

You will be surprised how willing someone is to help the person that bears all the responsibility. Honest and clear communication works. "Hey, this is my fault and I take responsibility for this situation. However, I do believe you have the skillset to help me find a solution." You will be amazed at how far people will go to help you when you put them in a position to be a hero. Not only does the problem get solved, but you are also increasing your bond and building confidence in those around you. More importantly, everybody moves forward.

Not everyone can be the superman or superwoman you are, but they would love to tell the story of the time they helped the superhero.

Dissolve

Perhaps, the most fatal form of fault as it pertains to growth and success is the dissolving of fault. Sweeping it under the rug and acting like it never happened. Right now, you can think of someone in your life that always acts like "It's all good," after an argument or discrepancy. You are still bothered by it and they pretend not to be.

What happens over time? The unresolved issues swept under the rug become a mountain between you and the person or between you and a goal. You may mentally try to avoid a situation, because you do not want to upset someone or because you do not to deal with it, not realizing that unresolved issues are poison. The longer you sit on them, the quicker they kill you from the inside. The longer you hold onto the grenade, the more apt you are to be caught in the explosion.

Do yourself a favor and allow nothing to be swept under the rug. This does not mean you have to argue and confront every situation, but when something needs attention, be sure you communicate to the other person you need to set aside some time to discuss the situation. If it is you sweeping issues under the rug, you need to set aside time to fix yourself. Remember, people only sweep issues under your rug if you let them. If you make them take accountability for the mess they are making in your life, they will soon find somewhere else to take their problems.

Stand firm and keep your house clean.

Criticism

Fault and criticism often go hand in hand. Most people fear both. But not champions, not you. Those with a Wintality understand that criticism comes with the territory. Aspiring speakers often approach me after a show or a broadcast and discuss with me their view on how cool it must be to travel and speak. I always listen and offer advice on how they can do the same. Though everything may appear like a fairy tale to them, I remind them that the Spotlight does not just magnify who you are; it exposes all your flaws for the world to see.

I do not tell them that to discourage them; I would just be doing them a disservice if I allowed them to be blind-sided by that truth. The reason many people remain at the level they are at in any walk of life is the fear of criticism. People fear being told they did not do a good job.

In all my years of athletics and public speaking, I have learned a valuable lesson – those who have walked in your shoes will seldom criticize what you are doing. They will assist you by helping you avoid the same mistakes they made. Those who are the most critical of you, often have never done what you are attempting to do. The view is a lot different on the sideline watching.

As is the case with fault, you have to learn to view criticism from a different perspective. Regardless of the intent of the criticism, you ultimately decide what you hang on to. First, learn to applaud yourself for being in a position worthy of criticism. No one criticizes people or situations that aren't relevant to anything. By the very definition, the fact you are being criticized means you are important enough for someone to watch what you are doing.

Once you grasp that, you can look at criticism as a grocery store. Mostly when we grocery shop, we go in there looking for particular items and often pick up a couple of things we did not expect to buy, but want or need anyway. There are rows of items, and each store has the same staples, but differing products or types of each product. When you go to the supermarket, you do not have to buy anything. You can just look around or you can purchase what you desire. When you leave, you take your items and forget about what's behind you in the store. You know that if you go back, those items will still be there.

Criticism is the same way. On the path to anything worthwhile, you will be filled with options of criticisms. Some people offer good advice; some just throw garbage at you (the junk food of the criticism market) and everything in between. Approach criticism like you do a grocery list. Know in advance the advice you need and seek it from people with a great track record (the good brands) and be open to receiving extra advice. Don't take anything with you that you do not need.

If you do not like honey buns and Twinkies, you do not avoid the supermarket simply because those desserts are for sale. You just don't buy those items. View criticism like groceries you don't like. Just because it's offered, doesn't mean you have to take it with you.

When you take that mentality, you are much more open to criticism, because you are not looking to avoid words and prolong success; you are looking for advice that can get you to your destination.

Julian Placino, host of the Pathways to Success podcast, built a career in recruiting by helping others find their dream jobs. Though he could give you the ins and outs of recruiting, what stuck out to me is the way he handles and advises those he helps with criticism and rejection. From the time I met Julian, I wondered how he remained so positive. When I asked him about handling rejection, which is a large facet of recruiting, I asked him, "Do you ever get down when you get rejected?" He said, "Are you kidding me? I love to get criticized or told no if they tell me why." I sat there shocked, not understanding how anyone could spin that into a positive.

He continued, "When I get told no or turned down by someone in a high position, they are providing me with free advice. To get that kind of feedback from someone in these positions is invaluable." It is mindsets like that, a reframing of a perceived negative word, that allows Julian to help people all over the world, and that same mindset will allow you to embrace the spotlight of your cause.

WINTALITY ACTION STEP: Which of the perspectives of fault do you rely on most frequently? Write a list of the most common situations you use them in and write a new list of what you will do next time you are in that situation.

RISE

"The greatest accomplishment is not in never falling, but in rising again after you fall." – Vince Lombardi

-12-

Leading the Pack

"Leadership is an ever-evolving position."
- Mike Krzyzewski

We all have an idea in mind of what a leader is. If I asked you to define the characteristics of a leader, you'd probably mention assertiveness, confidence, preparedness, patience, or a myriad of other leadership qualities. In my seminars, when I ask the same question, I get a lot of those correct answers. Answers to the next question I often ask is one of the principle reasons for me writing this book.

I ask audiences to name a leader. Many say their boss or upper management, the captain of their team, their spouse in the household, or team lead in their division. Very few answer the question with their own name. Conversely, often, I meet with members of upper management or CEO's of organizations who deem themselves leaders, but my corresponding conversation with their subordinates reveals otherwise.

There's a big difference in bosses and leaders. Boss is a position. Leadership is an earned respect. Bosses can be leaders, and leaders can and often become bosses, but they are not always synonymous. You will often find the difference in the two for the simple fact that bosses use their title to throw their authority and impose their methodology on those underneath them. You most likely had a boss or coach who operated in that manner.

Leaders demonstrate through action what needs to be done and others want to follow them. Do you see the difference? Forcing others based on title versus showing others through example. Which do you think garners the best results?

Bosses often try to prove their worth via their position or expertise. How often have you questioned a philosophy or task handed to you at your company only to be told: "BECAUSE I SAID SO?" Bosses' number one goal is often to remain on top; leaders' goals are to move the company or team forward.

Do you have a boss mindset or that of a leader? Is your goal to prove how great you are or to do what's necessary to get the greatest results? Do you want to be feared or would you rather be respected? Would you rather people tuck their tail between their legs and follow you or triumphantly run with you in the direction you are heading?

Bosses may drive you to get temporary results via rewards or fear, but leaders will make you want to perform at your peak for yourself and for the leader. In doing so, you get stronger and longer lasting results.

If we are honest with ourselves, in various aspects of our lives, we have seeped into "boss" mode and told ourselves we were leaders. Here's the truth. You are a leader. The question you must answer is this – "Where are you leading people?"

Whether or not you realize it, someone is watching you and being influenced by you. Remember, leadership is earned. That does not mean you are a good leader. Have you ever had a colleague or friend who gossips nonstop and constantly finds everything wrong with everyone? What happens to those that hang around that person? The negativity rubs off on the group. That person is a leader; he or she is just leading people the wrong way.

Every person is a leader, but not every person is a progressive leader. Wintality leaders are progressive and share a few common characteristics, though their approaches may be different. In understanding you are a leader, look at these qualities and see if they accurately represent you, and if not, see how you can improve on them to ensure you are leading your tribe the right way.

No deviation from the standard

Words can lie; actions can too, but patterns always reveal the truth of who someone is. As a general rule of thumb, most people will give you the lowest common denominator of what you will accept. If you do not value yourself or respect yourself, they will not either. They will perform for you at the lowest bar you set. That bar is not set by your words; it is set by your consistent actions.

If you deviate from the standards of what you ask of others by lowering the bar personally, you cannot expect people to live up to it again when you attempt to raise it. Why? Because they have witnessed you operating at a lower standard.

Case in point, think about a time you frequented a restaurant, supermarket, or fast food establishment with an item you consistently purchase. Over time, you get used to receiving that item for that predetermined price. One day, the price drops dramatically for a period, and you get used to the new low price. After a set period, the price goes up to what you originally paid, and what do you do? You pause, right? Why? Originally, you were ok with the original price, but once you get accustomed to getting it at a lower price, the original price seemed too high.

That is the mindset of most people when it comes to sweat equity. If they see you deviate from high standards, they will often see no reason to perform at higher standards when you try to raise them again because they know you can operate below them. To remain a great leader, you have to remain consistent with everyone, including yourself.

Legendary coaches are consistent in their approach to all players. They treat no one different, from the star to the bench warmers. Everyone knows what to expect. By establishing a standard, everyone is clear on those expectations and can confidently follow, knowing the system is fair to all. Don't you want your hard work to be rewarded if you outwork and outperform others? Your tribe wants the same thing from you.

Don't try and lead at everything

Great leaders know what they are good at and what they are not good at. While they try to improve on their weaknesses, an ultimate attribute of a great leader is to play on their strengths and surround themselves with people whose skillset compliments their weaknesses. They do not feel the need to know everything; they feel the need to do what they're good at and help others around them succeed by doing what they are best at.

Think of yourself as the driver of your vehicle in rush hour traffic. Every day, you know where you need to get, though people are on all sides of you, speeding up, breaking, and changing lanes. You know you need to keep your eyes forward to make sure you do not wreck or hit someone in front of you. You need to make sure you do not hit others in your blind spot when changing lanes. Which would be more productive: a) taking your eyes off the road to check your blind spot for traffic before switching lanes, or b) have a friend (or blind spot alert lights in your side mirrors) to warn you when someone is in the area you cannot see?

Having help will allow you to focus on moving the vehicle forward. Too often in life, many try to look around and cover their weaknesses (blind spots), while trying to move forward with their strengths. A great leader understands that he or she has blind spots. That same leader also understands people are gifted in the areas that the leader is not…someone to cover your blind spots. When you do not feel the need to be the best at everything, you open yourself to the ability to have great people around you while you become the best at something.

In an orchestra, all instruments make sounds at different frequencies so that, together, they cover the entire sound spectrum. The result is a pleasant harmony for the listener. What would happen if all the instruments made the same sound? The soundwaves would crash together, resulting in a jumbled noise that no one would want to listen to. Though some instruments may be more prominent to a listener, each instrument has a vital part of covering its sound frequency and contributing to the whole. As a great leader, it is your job to find the strengths in others that compliment your weaknesses, so that everyone can move forward without crashing into each other or swerving in each other's lanes.

Be willing to play any position

A great leader knows it is not the position he or she is in that matters; it is the direction and the outcome that the team is getting. As a committed leader, you have to commit to doing what's necessary, not just what you want to be doing.

Sometimes, a leader must lead by example; you may have to go show your team how to sell a product or dig in and show them you will do any job. Other times, your role may be to stand behind your team and serve as an assistant to their needs. Other times, you may need to be in front of your team, turn your back to the crowd, and pull your team along.

A great leader does not care about where they are; they just care that the team moves forward. They know they will have to serve as the head of the team, and other times, they may have to serve as the tail end of the team.

To be a great leader, your team must know you will lead if necessary or do the job of janitorial services if that is what's required – and everything in between. You will be amazed at how much harder people will work for you when they know you are not willing to ask anything of them that you would not do. By demonstrating that you will do their jobs, your team or tribe gets the comfort of knowing you realize the level of work involved for what you are asking them to do. When you will roll your sleeves up and work, others will be willing to work beside you.

Pursue the cause, not the credit

Why are great leaders willing to play any position to get the results? It is because leaders do what they do for the cause, not the credit. One of the main problems plaguing society today is that too many people want to be seen doing things more than they want to do the things they want to be seen for.

Do you want notoriety or want results? Most people do not understand that results are loud; they never lie. If you are working as hard as you say you are, the results will verify that. Eventually, the truth comes to light about who did the work, no matter how much others try to steal credit. Leaders do not care either way. A great leader knows that a win for the team is a win for the leader because the mission is being accomplished. Many great leaders get joy in the team feeling like they did the work. That feeling of accomplishment pushes the team to work even harder, ultimately sustaining the mission and goal the leader set out to accomplish.

I have never met a great leader who set out to become a leader. They simply had a vision and worked to make it a reality, and along the way, people supported and joined in. Everyone wants to follow someone who knows where he or she is going.

Know your tribe

Great leaders may not start out by trying to have a team, but they know the members of their tribe once they assemble behind that leader. Just like a lion protects its pride, a leader knows the needs, wants, strengths, and weaknesses of his or her tribe. When you are in-tune with those that look up to you for leadership and direction, you make their well-being a priority.

The Buffalo Theory states that herds of buffalo only move as fast as the slowest member. The reasoning behind this is that, while buffalo understand the importance of moving in herds for protection, they equally understand they can only move as fast as the slowest members. Sadly, though Buffalo do their best to protect each other, they also understand that not everyone can ultimately keep up. Eventually, some older or weaker Buffalo will pass away or be intercepted by predators. The goal of the Buffalo is to retain as many of the herd as possible at all times.

As a leader, you have to realize not everyone moves as fast as you. Sometimes, you may have to work quickly, but as a rule of thumb, don't leave the tribe that is dependent on you. Don't leave a team that is following you. Learn the people that support you. What drives them? What are their fears? When you can learn what drives them and help them overcome adversities, you can get the slowest members of your team to improve and move quicker, and the entire team gains momentum and moves toward the results you are after.

A motivated fearless team with unified momentum results directly from its leader. You can unleash those leadership qualities and lead your tribe towards an objective or ideal that benefits everyone involved in pursuing your overall vision.

The Anchor and the Sail

If I asked you which is more important, the Anchor or the Sail in a boat, how would you respond? You may say the sail since it sets the direction and speed of the boat. You might answer with the anchor since it keeps the boat in a solid position during storms. There is no right or wrong answer to the question, but as a leader, you have to be both the anchor and the sail.

Understand that your crew is looking to you to set the sails, the direction, and assure them you know where you are going. They rely on you to set the plan in motion and drive the team forward. By the same token, no one wants to be thrown around when the storms and adversities hit. When a problem arises, they need to trust you are an anchor, or strong foundation, that will not be swayed or pushed around. In times of panic, people need to look at someone who is calm, collected, and grounded.

As you continue to develop your leadership qualities, focus on having the swiftness of a sail, the steadiness of an anchor, and your crew will be more than willing to help row the boat.

WINTALITY ACTION STEP: Make a list of your leadership qualities and a list of your blind spots. Now, beneath each, write down who follows you because of your qualities and who can you recruit to cover your blind spots.

-13-
Letting Go

"He who knows that enough is enough will always have enough." – Lao Tzu

One of the greatest tragedies is watching a peak performer who does not know their time is up. We witness superstar athletes play well past their prime to a point where our last memories are not of their highlights, championships, and MVP's, but of the painstaking view of watching them try to continue to do what they love, far after their time has passed. Eventually, the teams must part ways with the legend in an unceremonious manner because the team must move on.

The same can be said of some peak performers at a job. Some people outlive their glory days and to remain relevant, continue to try to match their former self until ultimately the company must part ways and release the employee.

With a Wintality, both as a leader and as a lion, you have to come to grips with the fact that nothing lasts forever.

While this may seem like a sad swan song to some, those with a Wintality see the benefit and understand the positive attributes of letting go.

As a peak performer, your engine works faster than others, and you can go a lot further than most people. However, you cannot hold on to dead weight. Eventually, you have to let go. Have you ever seen a NASA rocket ship take off? When it takes off in a fiery blaze, the rocket ship sits on a large carrier surrounded by two silos, full of fuel. The fuel silos are in place because the rocket needs them to break through the atmosphere and gravitational pull of the earth. Eventually, the fuel containers run out of fuel – they have fulfilled their purpose. They were there for the rocket, they helped the rocket, but what happens if the rocket did not detach itself from the empty fuel containers?

They would all fall back to the earth, would they not? However, what was the rocket's purpose? The purpose was to reach space. To do so, the rocket understands that, at a certain point, it has to detach itself from its surroundings to reach new heights. The rocket knows when to let go.

During your life, you will be surrounded by good people and good situations and not so good people and bad situations. One thing is for certain – all things come to an end. Just as beginning with the end in mind is a solid business strategy when creating a company, understanding that your goal is to reach the finish line, not continue to run past it, is a vital part of success.

Am I suggesting you should stop when you get to the finish line or the goal? No. What I am asking you to do is realize that you started out with a goal, a plan, and a team to help you reach that certain goal. Once you reach it, you should always set a larger goal, climb a bigger mountain. However, to do so means you must look at those around you. Though your team or situation may have got you to the current goal, there is no guarantee they are equipped to take you to the next level. Not everyone was meant to stay with you on greater journeys; in fact, not everyone even wants to.

Not that you should use people. That is the antithesis of Wintality. A true Wintality is helping people get to their destination in pursuit of the one you are after. You should know your finish line. Yes, the goal is to cross the finish line and then to sign up for a new race, not to continue the race you have finished.

Too many people love the thrill of being in the game, so to speak, so much they forget the objective and run clear past their finish line. In the marathons and triathlons I compete in, the roads are marked and cleared so we can safely compete on the city streets. What would happen if I ran through the finish line down the major streets and highways? There would be an accident that wouldn't end well for me. What was the problem? The problem was that I trained for a certain distance, and the race officials prepared to keep me safe for that agreed upon distance. To run past the designated end point, means I am outrunning the system designed to protect me.

This happens when we don't know when to stop. You hear stories of gamblers in Vegas who get up big in their winnings and feel the need to roll the dice once more and lose it all. If they would have had a goal when to stop, they may still have money. We live in a society that tells us to go faster, get more, and do it one more time - but society is not always in line with our goals and objectives.

Every ship in the ocean ultimately takes its last voyage. If you hang on too long, you go down with the ship. This is why it is vital that you remember what you are after and when you get it, pause, recalibrate and set a new goal, a new target, or build a new ship.

Knowing when to let go also serves another purpose. It allows you to reach new heights you cannot reach if you are tied down. Think of yourself as a helium balloon. When you're filled with helium, you are meant to rise. You cannot fill yourself up; you need others to help you. Balloons are attached to a string while they are being filled up so they do not prematurely float off. This foundation is good for the balloon. However, at a certain point, the balloon is filled with helium, and that same string that gave the balloon stability, now prevents the balloon from soaring.

No matter how high you soar, you can never rise higher than that which you are tethered to. This means you have to be willing to cut the string when it is time to fly.

Are you still being tethered by people that used to be good for you? Are you remaining in jobs, careers, or companies that used to fuel your growth? Are you in a position or environment that used to progress your life? Do those same people, places, or positions still move you forward? Too often, we feel guilty for leaving others behind that helped us get to a certain position or level.

While it is true people might feel slighted when you rise, those that truly had your best interest at heart want to see you succeed. Those that didn't, well, let's just say it is a good thing you are not being tied down by those balloon poppers.

Take time at different phases in life to see if your situation is building you and prepping you for flight or if it is holding you back. Look at all the potential tethers, most notably the person in the mirror. More often than not, we sabotage our flight out of a strange loyalty to remaining grounded with those that helped prepare us to fly.

How would you feel if your best friend approached you in dire need of some financial assistance to help with a family situation? You no doubt worked hard for your money and had bills to pay, but sensing their need, loan them the money.

A week later, the friend calls you to tell you about the amazing vacation they took, sends pictures of the unforgettable opportunity, and does not mention the money you lent them. Would you not be angry that you put time, energy, and resources into putting that person in a position to take care of what they needed to take care of because it seemed like they needed your help? On top of that, they squandered away your hard work and resources!

That is how people feel that see your potential and watch you squander it away. Plainly put, you owe it to the people that are there for you to reach immense levels of success. Rising, even if it is alone, isn't the most selfish thing you could do; it is what you owe to the people that helped you prepare.

As with lions, the gunner (the fastest lion in the pride) owes it to the pride to go out alone and catch the gazelle that the entire pride spent hours circling and pushing toward that lion. The pride organizes and helps because they understand that, by doing their part, they are putting the fastest lion in a position to catch the prey they all benefit from.

If the pride spends hours selecting prey, stalking, attacking, and funneling the selected target toward the lion, only for the lioness to decide she wants to hang out with the pride, instead of going ahead by herself and performing her job, everyone suffers.

You owe it to those around you to succeed. You owe it to the environment that made you who you are to succeed, regardless if it was a good environment or bad environment. Finally, you owe it to yourself to know when to let go, leave the past behind, and sprint toward your destiny.

No Tear Goodbyes

Goodbyes are hard on those that spent much time together. The stronger the bond, the harder the goodbye. It need not be that way. Future hall of famer, Kobe Bryant, knew at the beginning of the 2015-2016 NBA season this was his final season. Kobe, the ultimate competitor, and arguably one of the greatest basketball players to play the game, could do something in his final season he seldom did before. He could smile. He could enjoy it. By understanding that his career was coming to an end, he got to enjoy the last season with his teammates. Fans flocked to watch Kobe play his final games in their arenas, wanting to watch a legend play his final games.

Because they knew the end was coming before the season started, the team could make sure they gave their all the entire season. They cherished the 82 games together. Kobe's final game was a historic game in which he led his team to victory and scored an astounding 60 points in a thrilling game with everyone in the Staples Center on their feet and everyone around the world glued to their TV watching Kobe go out in style.

After the game, he thanked the fans and was asked by the announcer if he would consider another season, to which Kobe responded, "No way, I'm done." I am sure Kobe will miss the game, but by knowing when it was time to walk away, knowing where his finish line was, he, with his teammates and family, didn't have to suffer from the "I wish I would have done more" syndrome that haunts many people. Kobe could leave it all on the court, and all of us got to revel in his final game and watch a legend retire and move on to greater things.

In the same manner, your goodbyes need not be sad. Whether it is a team, a job, or whatever it may be, communicate in the beginning about your goals and finish lines. Defined finish lines help others to cherish the time together and the momentum allows each to accomplish more in that time period.

When it's all said and done, cross your finish line and sign up for a new race. Months after his final game of his NBA Career, Kobe was on a new team, fueled with the same competitive fire by announcing his new company, BryantStibel, was joining the New York Stock Exchange with a $100-million-dollar venture capital fund.

Those with a wintality understand that saying goodbye to one opportunity is opening the door to the start of a greater opportunity. Cross your finish line, celebrate, and then find a new race.

WINTALITY ACTION STEP: Write down someone or something that's tethering you and preventing you from soaring to a new level.

You know what you need to do.

-14-
Tao of Wintality

"Show class, have pride and display character. If you do, winning takes care of itself." – Paul Bryant

Water is, perhaps, the most important resource on the planet and consequently one of the greatest teachers regarding maintaining a Wintality. Have you ever thought about the qualities of water and how you could benefit by acting similarly? I am not talking about the physical properties of hydrogen and oxygen, though our bodies comprise over 60% water. It's more about what water represents.

Necessity

We're made of it; we need it to survive, as does every life form on earth. Water is the DNA of the world. Without it, nothing thrives or grows; with it, growth potential is unlimited. Often, we take for granted how important water is. I remember the first time I returned from conducting mission work in Haiti, and all I could think about was getting a nice cold fresh bottle of water.

As water is a necessity for life, you, with your Wintality, can influence not only your growth, but the growth of all the people and the entire environment around you. Like pure water, when you are present with your full and authentic self, you become a lifeline to your situation and everyone in it.

Never forget what who you are

Water never forgets what it is. Though the environments it is in and what it endures may change, it remains water. At times of adversity, it turns to steam. In cold temperatures, it turns into ice. Though it may shift, change, and evolve to various states, it always stays true to what it is, water. No matter if you put it in a plastic bottle or the ocean, it is still the same – water.

You are a leader; you are a trailblazer. You will no doubt face the heat of adversity and a world turned cold in the times you must walk alone. What you cannot forget, no matter how tough life gets, is who you are and what you represent. Situations may change, you will evolve, but always remain true to who you are. That makes you unique; that is your greatest asset.

Momentum

A drop of water may seem harmless. A couple of drops of water may be an annoyance. A few more than drops than that and you may need an umbrella. However, what happens when you put many droplets of water together and give them momentum? The result is a Tidal wave capable of destroying cities.

Your goal is not to destroy cities, but with the same momentum, whether it's day by day, dollar by dollar, or step by step, you can create an epic presence that dominates whatever you are focused on conquering. Life truly is about momentum. With an ambitious mindset, you can get the ball rolling, allow others to join you, and ultimately see that your vision creates a wave of change and prosperity that drenches everything you touch.

Carve your own path

Water does not care about its opposition or how great its opponent is supposed to be. Some look at rocks and think it is impossible to break them. In every country in the world, water has carved its path through the tough rocks and terrain via river, stream, lake, or ocean. Day by day, it winds and runs and imposes its will on the land that seeks to control it. It is not hurried; it is not frightened, it has a mission and sees that it makes it to its intended destination.

Much like water, you cannot worry about what you are facing or what you have to endure to reach a goal. With the patience of water and a focused destination, you can carve your path through life. It is never about who or what you are facing; it is always about what's inside of you. The DNA to succeed is inside of you. Like water, it makes up your being and gives you the ultimate advantage in any scenario in life.

Alchemy

In ancient times, Alchemists were those who devoted their lives to learning how to turn base metals, such as lead, into precious metals, such as Gold. It required many years of training, study, focus, and work to become an alchemist and possess the mystical qualities that allowed the alchemist to turn lead to gold.

Now, whether you believe in the ability of someone to perform such a feat, the lessons apply today. Alchemists believed all things in the world were connected. The difference between lead and gold was simply one of immaturity. The purer (mature) they could make the lead, the sooner it turned to gold. Gold was the penultimate result of removing the impurities from a normal metal.

To accomplish this task, the alchemist had to have complete harmony in his mind, body, and soul. For without that harmony, impurities would remain and prevent the alchemist from creating gold.

You are an alchemist. You can turn a normal life into a golden life. You can take a regular adversity and create a golden result. Yes, it is about growth; yes, it is about learning, but ultimately, it is about you.

You have what it takes. You always have. Now it is time to shed the fear, chip away the doubt, chisel away the negative and false conditioning that has prevented you from reaching the heights you were destined to reach. With an unbreakable will, you must continue to pursue the mountain peaks of life and reach the finish lines far beyond those that most settle for.

Release inside you the masterpiece that exists. You will stumble, you will fall, but you will move forward. You are a lion - it is time to hunt and claim what's yours.

WINTALITY ACTION STEP: - Go Win!

"You had the power inside you all along."
– Glenda the Good Witch

WINTALITY

About the Author

Baylor Barbee is an American entrepreneur, author, and triathlete.

With an emphasis on peak performance, he pushes audiences to overcome adversities and surpass their goals through his speaking, professional development solutions, and books.

Baylor is an Amazon best-selling author and was named by the Dallas Convention & Visitors Bureau as one of the top 12 most influential African-Americans in Dallas.

A former Division 1 scholarship athlete, Baylor played football for Baylor University where he holds a B.B.A in Marketing & Entrepreneurship and a Master's Degree in Education.

Connect with Baylor at:

http://www.twitter.com/baylorbarbee
http://www.facebook.com/baylorbarbee
https://www.linkedin.com/in/baylorbarbee

http://www.BaylorBarbee.com

Never offer Service
   undervalue your time..
always package as a
Product. Solution. Pay
up front

What Really need __product__!

Tell em why they need
you.

Solution Based Products

Chief Diversity Officer

Untapped Market

- Diversity Market
- Events
- Access - NA

- Payoer ng
- warm lead
-

Will Send Sponsor level
what VAlue. Products
+ monetary donations

Trent Shelton

- Don't ask options, tell em what ~~offer~~ $750⁰⁰

- You choose photographer ..., not them

- Social Media King

- Ref. Photographers are slow, not biz SAVVY ... your differentiator.

- Only way will fail is if don't put forth consistent Effort failure

- List of idea of success

- List of things guarantee failure! (How many doing)

Made in the USA
Charleston, SC
01 March 2017

68058008R10118

- what can I chip away!